PROPERTY AND CASUALTY INSURANCE LICENSE EXAM PREP

The Masterclass with Clear-Cut Strategies, State-Specific Questions, and Detailed Explanations for a One-Shot Pass

Blueprint Institute

Summary

About the Author

Blueprint Institute is a pioneering company in professional study guides and test preparation, uniquely blending cutting-edge learning technologies with dynamic educational strategies. Established by a collective of certified teachers, digital learning experts and authors, our focus is crafting top-tier educational resources catering to learners across various age groups. Our mission is simple yet profound: transforming learning into an engaging, efficient, and universally accessible journey.

We are dedicated to empowering students with the knowledge and tools they need for academic success. Our approach combines the latest digital learning technology with proven educational methods, ensuring every learner can access top-quality resources.

Our name stands as a commitment to educational excellence and advancement. We are dedicated to ongoing research and developing novel teaching strategies, ensuring every learner can achieve their highest potential.

Join us in navigating a personalized educational path that paves the way to future success!

Introduction

Welcome to "Property and Casualty Insurance License Exam Prep: The Masterclass," an extensive guide meticulously crafted to prepare you for the Property and Casualty Insurance License Exam. As you embark on this journey, our structured guide will be your roadmap to understanding the intricacies of insurance policies and regulations, equipping you with the knowledge and skills necessary for your examination and professional success in the insurance industry.

This book is structured into seven distinct parts, each carefully designed to cover a comprehensive range of topics crucial for a thorough understanding of property and casualty insurance. Whether you are new to the field or a seasoned professional seeking to deepen your knowledge, this guide offers valuable insights into every aspect of insurance you need to master.

Part I: Understanding Insurance Fundamentals

We begin with the foundational elements of insurance, covering general concepts that underpin all types of insurance policies. This includes an introduction to basic insurance terminology, the structure of insurance contracts, and the differences between named peril and open peril policies. We will explore the critical roles of deductibles and liability limits in shaping insurance coverage. This part sets the stage by providing the essential principles governing the insurance industry.

Part II: Detailed Exploration of Insurance Types

Moving deeper, we delve into the specific types of property and casualty insurance, from residential to commercial, and the particularities of liability insurance. This section provides an in-depth look at different insurance products, including emerging areas like cyber insurance and traditional sectors such as marine and aviation insurance.

Part III: Policy Applications and Specific Coverage

Here, we examine specific insurance policy applications, detailing coverage options and policy exclusions. This part focuses on practical knowledge, such as understanding dwelling coverage under homeowner policies and covering risks like floods and earthquakes.

Part IV: Risk Management, Premiums, and Underwriting

Risk assessment and premium calculation are pivotal in the insurance process. This section breaks down the underwriting process, discussing how insurers assess risk and determine insurance premiums. You'll learn about coinsurance, the implications of pro-rata and short-rate cancellations, and the differences between actual cash value and replacement cost valuations.

Part V: Legal Framework, Claims, and Regulations

The insurance regulatory environment is complex and varies by state. This part covers the legal aspects of insurance, including state-specific regulations and the broader legal framework that impacts how policies are written, and claims are handled. We discuss the claims process from initial notice to resolution and fraud detection and dispute resolution strategies.

Part VI: Market Dynamics and Advanced Considerations

In this section, we explore the insurance market dynamics, including the role of regulatory bodies like the NAIC and the impact of technological advancements on insurance practices. This part is designed to inform you about current trends and future directions in the insurance industry.

Section II: Exam Preparation Finally, we focus on preparing you for the Property and Casualty Insurance License Exam. This section includes study tips, test-taking strategies, and a variety of practice questions designed to test your understanding and readiness for the exam.

To further enhance your preparation, the book includes two valuable bonuses:

1. **State-Specific Multiple-Choice Questions:** This bonus provides additional practice questions that focus on the specific regulations and practices of different states, helping you tailor your study to the requirements of the state where you will be taking your exam.

2. **Flashcards:** A set of detailed flashcards featuring key terms and concepts designed to help you study more effectively and reinforce your knowledge.

Through this structured approach, combining theoretical knowledge with practical applications and extensive exam preparation, "Property and Casualty Insurance License Exam Prep: The Masterclass" is not just a study guide—it is a comprehensive tool designed to guide you through every step of your learning journey, ensuring you are thoroughly prepared to pass your exam and excel in your career in the insurance industry.

This book is designed not just to prepare you for the exam but to equip you with a deep understanding of property and casualty insurance practices tailored to the specific requirements of the 2024-2025 exam cycle. Whether you are a new entrant into the world of insurance or a seasoned professional looking to certify or refresh your knowledge, this masterclass is structured to ensure a thorough preparation.

Using This Book Effectively:

- **Read Sequentially**: It's beneficial for those new to insurance to read the book from start to finish. This approach will build your knowledge progressively and contextually.

- **Topic-Specific Study**: If you are already familiar with certain aspects of insurance, you may focus on specific sections necessary for filling gaps in your knowledge.

- **Practice Makes Perfect**: Regularly test your knowledge using the practice questions and flashcards provided in the book. This will not only prepare you for the format of the exam but also reinforce your learning.

- **Stay Updated**: Given the dynamism of the insurance field, especially with state-specific regulations, supplement your study with the latest industry developments that might affect the exam content.

And now, enjoy the reading!

SECTION I
Theoretical Framework and Key Concepts.

This section serves as your gateway to understanding the broad landscape of property and casualty insurance, the critical role of licensing, and the structured process of the licensing exam. We aim to equip you with a robust foundation in universal insurance principles applicable across all states, preparing you for the exam and a successful career in the industry.

The insurance industry plays a vital role by providing financial protection against potential losses and liabilities. Property and casualty insurance, covering a wide range of policies that protect physical property and provide liability coverage for damages to others, is crucial in this sector. Professionals in this field need to stay informed about global economic conditions, technological advancements, natural disasters, and evolving regulatory environments, as these factors directly influence the dynamics of insurance.

Obtaining a property and casualty insurance license is more than a regulatory milestone; it establishes you as a knowledgeable and trustworthy professional. This certification signifies your commitment to professional excellence and ethical standards, enhancing clients' trust in your services.

The comprehensive licensing exam is designed to test your understanding of general and specific insurance laws, regulations, and practices. It covers the basics of insurance, property insurance, casualty insurance, and the various policy provisions. While the core principles are consistent across the United States, specific regulations can vary by state, adding complexity to your preparation.

As we delve deeper into this section, remember that the knowledge you gain here will build a solid base for your ongoing professional development in the insurance industry. Let's proceed with a clear focus on these foundational concepts, ensuring a comprehensive understanding and readiness for the challenges ahead. As we progress through this section, it's important to highlight that we will be addressing 50 fundamental topics essential for mastering the Property and Casualty Insurance License Exam. These topics have been thoughtfully divided into five broad categories, each designed to streamline your study process and enhance your understanding.

Every detail of this book has been meticulously crafted to offer maximum efficiency in your preparation. By organizing the content into clear, focused areas, we ensure that your study sessions are practical and comprehensive. This structure aids in easier absorption and retention of the material but also helps you navigate the complexities of the exam content more easily.

Our approach is to build a solid foundation covering all necessary property and casualty insurance aspects. We reinforce each concept with quizzes and practice questions (Section II) that prepare you for the challenges you will encounter on the exam. As you engage with each of these topics, you'll understand the core principles and advanced strategies essential for success in the exam and beyond.

Let's embark on this detailed exploration of the insurance landscape, confident that every element of this guide has been designed to enhance your learning experience and equip you with the knowledge and skills needed for a successful outcome.

PART I: UNDERSTANDING INSURANCE FUNDAMENTALS

General Insurance Concepts

Insurance is a fundamental tool for managing risk and providing security. Insurance involves transferring a potential financial loss from an individual or business to an insurance company in exchange for a premium. This exchange is governed by the principles of risk pooling, where many entities pay into a fund managed by the insurer, which then uses these contributions to compensate those who suffer covered losses.

Understanding these general insurance concepts is crucial for anyone entering the property and casualty insurance field. It forms the foundation upon which more detailed and specific knowledge is built. Insurance operates on several key principles:

1. **Indemnity**: This principle ensures that policyholders receive compensation for their losses, bringing them back to their financial position before the loss, without the opportunity to profit from the insurance claim.

2. **Utmost Good Faith**: The insurer and the insured are expected to act honestly and not mislead or withhold critical information from one another.

3. **Proximate Cause**: Identifies the primary cause of loss and determines whether it is covered under the insurance policy terms.

4. **Subrogation**: After compensating for a loss, the insurer may assume the legal rights of the insured to pursue third parties that may be responsible for the loss.

These principles guide the creation and enforcement of all insurance contracts, ensuring that the system works fairly and efficiently for all parties involved. By mastering these basic concepts, prospective agents and brokers can better understand their responsibilities and the protections offered to policyholders, laying a solid groundwork for further study and professional practice in property and casualty insurance.

Insurance Basics

The basic concepts that govern how policies are designed, priced, and sold are at the foundation of the insurance industry. Understanding these basics is essential for any insurance professional, particularly in the field of property and casualty insurance.

Insurance policies are formal agreements between an insurer and the insured, where the insurer agrees to compensate the insured for specific losses in exchange for a premium. These agreements are contingent upon several fundamental elements:

1. **Policyholder**: The individual or entity who owns the policy and is entitled to coverage.

2. **Premium**: The amount paid by the policyholder to the insurance company. Premiums are calculated based on the risk associated with insuring the policyholder and the coverage provided.

3. **Coverage Limit**: The maximum amount the insurance company will pay in the case of a claim. Limits are set based on the potential financial impact of the risk being insured against and the policyholder's preferences.

4. **Deductible**: A cost-sharing mechanism where the policyholder is responsible for paying a specified amount of a claim before the insurer's coverage kicks in. Deductibles can influence the cost of the premium and encourage policyholders to prevent minor claims.

These basic elements are integral to all types of insurance policies and play a critical role in the dynamics of risk management. By setting clear and mutually agreed upon terms, insurance policies ensure that both parties—the insurer and the insured—understand their obligations and the conditions under which coverage is adequate. This mutual understanding helps to streamline claims processing. It enhances the overall efficiency of the insurance market, providing a stable economic environment for both personal and business endeavors.

Understanding Insurance Policy Components: Declarations, Insuring Agreements, Conditions, Exclusions, Endorsements

A comprehensive understanding of the individual components of an insurance policy is crucial for insurance professionals and policyholders. Each component plays a distinct role in defining the coverage provided and both parties' obligations.

1. **Declarations**: Often referred to as the "dec page," this part of the policy summarizes the essential information. It includes the name of the insured, the address, the policy period, amounts of coverage, and premiums. This section provides a quick reference that outlines who is covered under the policy, what is covered, the limits of coverage, and other key details that are specific to the policyholder.

2. **Insuring Agreements**: This segment of the policy spells out the insurer's promise to pay and under what circumstances. It defines the scope of coverage the policy provides, detailing the risks covered and the type of losses the insurer agrees to indemnify. This is the core of the insurance contract, specifying what the insurer promises to do in exchange for the premium paid by the insured.

3. **Conditions**: These stipulations specify the obligations of the policyholder and the insurer. Conditions must be met for the coverage to be legally enforceable. They might include requirements for reporting losses, cooperating during investigations, and how to file a claim. These conditions ensure that the policy operates effectively and both parties fulfill their roles responsibly.

4. **Exclusions**: Critical for defining the policy's limitations, exclusions detail what is not covered by the policy. Understanding exclusions is essential because it clarifies the boundaries of the insurance coverage, helping to set realistic expectations for what events or damages are not covered under the terms of the policy.

5. **Endorsements**: Also known as riders, endorsements modify the original terms of the policy. They can be used to add or delete coverage and adjust premiums. Endorsements allow for customization of a policy to fit the specific needs of the insured, reflecting changes in risk exposure or requirements of the policyholder.

By mastering the details of these components, insurance professionals can better design, sell, and manage policies, ensuring that they meet the specific needs of their clients while maintaining clarity and understanding of the coverage provided.

Named Peril vs. Open Peril Policies: Definitions and Differences

Understanding the distinction between named and open peril policies is crucial for insurance professionals and policyholders alike, as it defines the scope of risk coverage under a property and casualty insurance policy.

1. **Named Peril Policies**: These policies specify exactly which perils the insurance policy covers. Common examples of named perils include fire, theft, windstorm, and hail—risks explicitly listed in the policy documents. Coverage under a named peril policy is limited to the damages caused by the perils specifically identified; any loss resulting from a peril not listed is not covered. This type of policy puts the onus on the policyholder to prove that a loss resulted from one of the named perils, making it a more restrictive and often less expensive option.

2. **Open Peril Policies**: Also known as all-risk policies, open peril policies offer a broader range of coverage. These policies cover all risks of loss that are not explicitly excluded in the policy documents. Exclusions in open peril policies might include events like war, nuclear disaster, or wear and tear. The key advantage of an open peril policy is its comprehensive nature, which provides coverage unless the peril is explicitly excluded. This shifts the burden to the insurer to

prove that an exclusion applies if they deny a claim, offering more extensive protection to the policyholder.

The choice between named and open peril policies often depends on the policyholder's specific needs, risk tolerance, and budget. Named peril policies may be suitable for those seeking more affordable coverage with an understanding of their particular risks. In contrast, open peril policies are preferable for those requiring more comprehensive coverage against a wider array of potential risks. Understanding these differences is essential for tailoring insurance solutions that accurately meet the needs and expectations of clients while providing clear communication about what is and is not covered.

The Role of Deductibles in Insurance Policies

Deductibles play a crucial role in the structure of insurance policies, influencing both the cost and the coverage of the insurance plan. Understanding how deductibles work is essential for anyone involved in the insurance industry, from policyholders to agents.

A deductible is the amount of money a policyholder agrees to pay out-of-pocket before the insurance company begins paying its share of the costs for a covered loss. This feature is a fundamental part of the risk-sharing agreement between the insurer and the insured. Deductibles can vary significantly depending on the type of insurance, the insurer's offerings, and the policyholder's willingness to share in the risk of potential losses.

1. **Risk Management:** Deductibles are a form of self-insurance where the policyholder assumes a portion of the risk. This arrangement helps to mitigate moral hazard, as policyholders with higher deductibles may be more motivated to prevent losses and minimize the number of small claims.

2. **Premium Costs:** Generally, the higher the deductible, the lower the premium. By choosing a higher deductible, policyholders can reduce their regular insurance costs. This trade-off requires balancing the immediate savings on premiums and the potential need to cover larger out-of-pocket expenses in the event of a claim.

3. **Claims Process:** Deductibles also influence the claims process. The deductible amount is subtracted from the claim payment when a loss occurs. For example, if a policyholder has a $500 deductible and incurs a covered loss of $2,000, the insurer would pay $1,500 after the deductible amount is applied.

Understanding deductibles is crucial for policyholders to make informed decisions about their insurance coverage. It allows them to choose a level of risk they are comfortable with while managing their insurance expenses effectively. For insurance professionals, clearly explaining the role and impact of deductibles to clients ensures transparency. It helps build trust by aligning the insurance coverage with the client's needs and risk tolerance.

Limits of liability are a fundamental aspect of insurance contracts, determining the maximum amount an insurer will pay for a covered claim under a policy. These limits are crucial for both the insurer and the insured, as they define the extent of coverage provided and help manage financial exposure for both parties.

1. **Protection for Policyholders**: Limits of liability are essential for policyholders because they specify the maximum amount they can expect in compensation after a covered loss. This knowledge allows individuals and businesses to plan and prepare for potential financial risks and to purchase sufficient coverage to meet their needs. For example, knowing the limits in auto insurance can help a policyholder understand how much they would receive for vehicle repairs or medical expenses after an accident.

2. **Risk Management for Insurers**: Setting liability limits is a critical risk management tool for insurers. It helps them control the potential maximum loss they could face from a single claim or series of claims. By capping their financial obligations, insurers can ensure their ability to cover all claims filed by all their policyholders without jeopardizing their financial stability.

3. **Premium Calculations**: The limits of liability also influence the premium rates charged by insurers. Generally, higher liability limits result in higher premiums, as the insurer takes on a greater risk of financial loss. Policyholders must balance their need for adequate coverage with the cost of higher premiums, which can be particularly important in areas prone to high-cost claims, such as liability insurance for businesses.

4. **Legal Requirements**: In many cases, limits of liability are not just a matter of personal preference but are also influenced by legal requirements. Certain types of insurance, such as auto liability insurance, may have minimum limit requirements set by state law, ensuring enough coverage to pay for damages or injuries that the policyholder might cause to others.

Understanding how liability limits work, how they affect insurance coverage, and how they can be adjusted to meet individual needs is crucial for anyone involved in the insurance market. This understanding ensures that policyholders comply with legal standards and are adequately protected according to their personal risk profiles.

With this solid grounding, you are well-prepared to delve into more detailed and specific property and casualty insurance aspects in the book's subsequent sections.

PART II: DETAILED EXPLORATION OF INSURANCE TYPES

Property Insurance Basics

Property insurance is a critical component of the insurance industry. It is designed to provide financial reimbursement to the owner or renter of a structure and its contents in case of damage or theft. Property insurance can include homeowners insurance, renters insurance, flood insurance, and insurance covering commercial buildings. Understanding the basics of property insurance is essential for anyone entering the property and casualty field, as it covers a wide range of potential risks and protections.

Property insurance policies are typically structured to cover the risk of damage from fire, water, theft, and other hazards. Each policy usually specifies what types of damage are covered, and, importantly, what types are excluded. For example, most standard property insurance policies cover damage caused by fire or storm but may exclude natural disasters like floods and earthquakes unless specifically added as coverage through endorsements.

The fundamental purpose of property insurance is to help individuals and businesses recover financially from unexpected losses to property. This insurance plays a vital role in the economy by providing the security necessary for individuals and companies to invest in real estate and personal property with confidence. Insurers assess various factors to determine the risks associated with insuring a property, including location, the value of the property, the materials used in construction, and the likelihood of events like theft or natural disasters occurring in the area.

For insurance professionals, understanding these basics is crucial for effectively assessing risks, setting premiums, and designing policies that meet the diverse needs of policyholders. This foundational knowledge also helps advise clients on risk management strategies and navigate claims when losses occur.

Types of Property Insurance

Diving deeper into property insurance, we encounter various specialized forms catering to distinct needs and risks associated with different properties. These types provide coverage tailored to specific situations, from residential homes to large commercial complexes, each with unique challenges and requirements.

1. **Homeowners Insurance**: This is perhaps the most familiar form of property insurance, providing coverage for damage to a residence and its contents and liability protection for injuries on the property. Homeowners insurance typically covers many perils, including fire, storm damage, theft, and vandalism. It also often includes liability coverage that protects the homeowner from financial loss if they are legally responsible for injury to another person or damage to another person's property.

2. **Renters Insurance**: Designed for individuals leasing or renting their living space, this insurance covers personal property within the rented property and may provide liability coverage similar to homeowners insurance. Renters must understand that while the landlord may insure the building, the protection does not extend to the tenant's personal property.

3. **Commercial Property Insurance**: This type covers buildings and personal property owned by a business. It provides a broader range of coverage, including building, equipment, inventory, furniture, and even loss of income resulting from the business being temporarily unable to operate due to damage from a covered loss.

4. **Condo Insurance**: Specifically designed for condominium owners, this insurance fills in the gaps left by the condo association's master policy, which typically covers the building and common areas. Condo insurance covers the unit's interior and the owner's personal property and personal liability.

5. **Flood Insurance**: Often excluded from standard property insurance policies, flood insurance must be purchased separately and is highly recommended or required in flood-prone areas. This insurance covers damage to the building and contents due to flooding, which is not covered under most standard homeowners' policies.

6. **Earthquake Insurance**: Similar to flood insurance, earthquake coverage is typically excluded from standard property policies and must be purchased separately. It provides coverage for damage caused by earthquakes, which can be indispensable in earthquake-prone regions.

7. **Landlord Insurance**: Designed for individuals who own properties that they rent out, landlord insurance covers the building, loss of rental income, and sometimes liability for injuries that occur on the property, distinct from normal homeowners insurance which does not cover tenants.

Understanding these various types of property insurance allows insurance professionals to better serve their clients by recommending the right type of coverage based on their specific circumstances and the risks associated with the property they own or occupy. Each type has its nuances and conditions, which must be clearly understood to manage risks and provide adequate coverage effectively. This knowledge is crucial for passing the licensing exam and practical application professionally, ensuring clients receive the most appropriate and comprehensive coverage for their needs.

Homeowners insurance is a cornerstone of property insurance that provides homeowners with essential financial protection against various common perils. Understanding the scope and intricacies of homeowners insurance is crucial for insurance professionals, as it equips them to offer detailed advice and suitable coverage options to homeowners.

A typical homeowners insurance policy includes several key components:

1. **Dwelling Coverage**: This forms the core of homeowners insurance, providing funds to repair or rebuild the house in the event of damage from covered perils such as fire, windstorms, or hail. The amount of coverage is based on the estimated cost to rebuild the home, which can fluctuate with changes in construction costs.

2. **Other Structures Coverage**: This protects structures on the property that are not attached to the house, such as garages, sheds, and fences. Coverage limits for other structures are usually set as a percentage of the dwelling coverage.

3. **Personal Property Coverage**: This compensates for the loss of or damage to the homeowner's personal belongings, both within the home and outside, such as items stolen while traveling. Homeowners can choose between replacement cost or actual cash value coverage, the latter of which includes depreciation.

4. **Loss of Use Coverage**: If a covered disaster makes the home uninhabitable, this coverage pays for living expenses (like hotel bills or meals) beyond typical living costs, allowing the family to maintain a usual standard of living while repairs are made.

5. **Liability Insurance**: This protects against lawsuits for bodily injury or property damage that the policyholders or family members cause to other people. It also pays for damage caused by pets. Moreover, liability insurance covers legal defense costs if the homeowner is sued.

6. **Medical Payments Coverage**: This covers medical expenses if someone is injured on the homeowner's property or by the homeowner's pets, regardless of who is at fault. It is designed to prevent small claims from becoming more significant lawsuits.

Homeowners' insurance policies also come with deductibles, which are the amounts homeowners must pay out of pocket before the insurance coverage kicks in. Deductibles can vary significantly and can affect the premium of the policy. Policyholders often choose higher deductibles to lower their premium costs, but this increases their financial responsibility in the event of a claim.

Moreover, while homeowners insurance covers many perils, it does not cover all scenarios. Common exclusions include floods and earthquakes, for which homeowners must purchase separate policies.

For insurance professionals, offering a clear explanation of each component and how it functions within the policy is crucial. This helps homeowners make informed insurance decisions and protects them adequately against potential risks. As the housing market and environmental conditions evolve, the insurance industry must adapt, making continuous education about policy options and changes imperative for those in the field. This foundational understanding is essential for passing the licensing exam and practical application in advising clients effectively.

Commercial Property Insurance: Critical Coverage Points

Commercial property insurance is an indispensable safeguard for businesses, offering financial

protection against many risks that can affect their physical assets. This form of insurance is designed to cover buildings, equipment, inventory, furniture, and other valuable property owned by a company. Understanding the critical coverage points of commercial property insurance is essential for insurance professionals, as it enables them to provide tailored advice that aligns with the unique needs of each business client.

One of the foundational elements of commercial property insurance is the business's physical structure coverage. This includes the main building and any additional structures, providing protection against perils such as fire, explosions, storms, and vandalism. Significantly, the policy also extends to cover the contents of the building, which can include office equipment, computers, machinery, and raw materials, against similar risks.

Additionally, commercial property insurance often encompasses business interruption insurance, compensating for income lost due to the business being temporarily unable to operate following a covered loss. This aspect is crucial for maintaining financial stability and covering ongoing expenses like payroll and rent during periods of disruption.

Another critical component is liability protection, which covers legal fees and settlements if the business is held legally responsible for damage to third-party property or personal injury caused within the business premises. This coverage is vital in mitigating the potentially ruinous costs of lawsuits and legal claims.

Moreover, commercial property insurance policies are customizable with various endorsements that can be added to address specific risks associated with certain industries or activities. For instance, a business that relies heavily on electronic data may include data breach coverage. At the same time, another in a flood-prone area might add flood insurance, recognizing that standard policies typically exclude such coverage.

Discerning and recommending the appropriate mix of coverage options and endorsements is paramount for insurance professionals. This expertise ensures that business clients are protected against common perils and prepared for industry-specific risks, providing comprehensive coverage that supports the company's longevity and resilience. This high level of professional knowledge is critical for aiding clients effectively and upholding the insurance industry's standards and ensuring thorough risk management.

Casualty Insurance Basics

Casualty insurance plays a crucial role in individuals' and businesses' risk management strategies by providing financial protection against liability claims. This type of insurance is primarily concerned with covering the policyholder from losses stemming from injuries or damage to others or their property. Understanding the basics of casualty insurance is fundamental for insurance professionals, as it allows them to adequately assess and address the liability risks faced by their clients.

Casualty insurance encompasses a variety of coverage types, but most notably includes liability insurances such as auto liability, general liability, and workers' compensation. Each type of liability coverage is designed to protect against specific risks:

- **Auto Liability Insurance** covers damages and injuries caused by vehicle accidents where the policyholder is at fault.

- **General Liability Insurance** provides coverage for accidents, injuries, and negligence claims that occur on business premises or as a result of business operations.

- **Workers' Compensation** offers compensation for employees who get injured on the job, covering their medical expenses and a portion of their lost wages.

The key component of casualty insurance is its focus on legal liability. Policies typically cover the legal costs associated with defending a claim and any settlements or awards that are part of the covered incidents. This can include medical costs, legal fees, and other damages awarded in civil lawsuits.

For insurance professionals, a deep understanding of casualty insurance is vital for crafting policies that adequately protect clients against potential liabilities that could otherwise financially cripple them or their businesses. Professionals must navigate the nuances of liability risks and the legal landscape to ensure comprehensive coverage. This expertise not only safeguards clients but also bolsters the reputation of the professional as a trusted advisor in the insurance industry.

Types of Casualty Insurance

Casualty insurance is a broad category that encompasses several types of coverage, each designed to protect against specific risks associated with legal liabilities. This coverage is vital for managing the potential financial impact of accidents, injuries, and other liabilities that could otherwise result in significant financial loss for individuals and businesses. Here are some of the primary types of casualty insurance that insurance professionals need to be well-versed in to provide comprehensive risk management solutions to their clients:

1. **Professional Liability Insurance**: Errors and Omissions (E&O) insurance covers professionals against claims of inadequate work or negligent actions. It is essential for professionals such as architects, lawyers, accountants, and consultants, whose services could cause financial loss to clients if performed improperly.

2. **Employment Practices Liability Insurance (EPLI)** protects businesses from claims by workers that their legal rights as company employees have been violated. EPLI covers issues such as discrimination, wrongful termination, sexual harassment, and retaliation.

3. **Directors and Officers (D&O) Insurance**: This type of insurance protects the personal assets of corporate directors and officers, as well as their spouses, in the event they are personally sued by employees, vendors, competitors, investors, customers, or other parties, for actual or alleged wrongful acts in managing a company.

4. **Umbrella Insurance**: This extends coverage beyond the limits of an individual's other personal liability policies. It is not a standalone policy but acts as an extra layer of protection that kicks in when the underlying liability limits (such as those in homeowners or auto insurance) have been reached.

5. **Product Liability Insurance**: Businesses that manufacture, distribute, or sell products can be liable if these products cause harm or injury. Product liability insurance protects against claims related to manufacturing or selling products, including defects in design, manufacturing, and marketing (such as failure to warn of potential dangers).

6. **Cyber Liability Insurance**: As businesses increasingly rely on digital operations, the risk of cyber threats grows. Cyber liability insurance covers businesses against losses caused by cyber events, including data breaches, network damage, and cyber extortion demands.

Liability Insurance Basics for Businesses and Individuals

Liability insurance is essential for businesses and individuals as it protects against claims resulting from injuries and damage to people or property. Liability coverage is a crucial aspect of casualty insurance because it covers legal costs and payouts for which the insured might be responsible if found legally liable. Understanding liability insurance basics is vital for insurance professionals who need to guide their clients through complex risk landscapes.

1. **General Liability Insurance**: This is one of the most common types of liability insurance for businesses. It protects against financial loss due to bodily injury, property damage, medical expenses, libel, slander, defending lawsuits, and settlement bonds or judgments required during an appeal procedure. It's a foundational policy for any business as it covers the types of accidents in any setting.

2. **Personal Liability Insurance**: Often included in homeowners' policies, personal liability insurance covers individuals against claims of bodily injury or property damage caused to others. This type of insurance is critical for protecting individuals from the potential financial consequences of litigation resulting from accidents in their home or as a result of their actions.

3. **Business Owners Policy (BOP)**: Combining various types of liability protection, a BOP typically includes general liability as well as property insurance, business interruption insurance, and sometimes vehicle coverage. This bundled approach can provide cost-effective coverage tailored to specific needs for small to medium-sized businesses.

4. **Employer's Liability Insurance**: Part of workers' compensation insurance, employer's liability insurance protects businesses from financial loss if an employee suffers a job-related injury or disease that isn't covered under workers' compensation. It covers legal fees and related costs if the business is sued, including any resulting judgments or settlements.

5. **Professional Liability Insurance (PLI)**: Also known as Errors and Omissions (E&O) insurance, PLI is critical for professionals who engage in services or provide advice. It covers the legal costs and payouts for negligence, misrepresentation, violation of good faith, and inaccurate advice that might cause clients financial loss.

Understanding these various facets of liability insurance enables insurance professionals to assess accurately and manage the risks associated with their clients' activities. Whether advising individual clients or large businesses, insurance professionals must ensure their clients have adequate protection to cover potential liabilities, thereby safeguarding their financial stability and reputation. This comprehensive approach to liability insurance helps mitigate risks and enhances the client's trust in their insurance advisor's expertise and commitment to their protection.

Special Form Coverage: What It Entails and When It Applies

Special form coverage is a type of property insurance that provides a broader spectrum of protection compared to basic or broad-form coverage policies. Unlike named peril policies that only protect against specific risks listed in the policy, special form coverage generally insures against all risks of physical loss unless explicitly excluded. This inclusiveness makes it a highly desirable option for many policyholders seeking comprehensive asset protection.

1. **Coverage Scope**: Special form coverage is designed to offer the highest level of protection available in property insurance. It covers damage to buildings and personal property from almost all causes except those expressly excluded, such as floods, earthquakes, war, nuclear incidents, and intentional acts by the insured. This all-encompassing approach ensures that it is covered unless a risk is clearly excluded, which provides policyholders significant peace of mind.

2. **Common Exclusions**: While special form coverage is extensive, it is crucial to understand its exclusions to manage expectations and additional coverage needs. Typical exclusions in special form policies may include governmental action, faulty workmanship, pollution, and wear and tear. Recognizing these exclusions is vital for policyholders to consider additional riders or separate policies to protect against their specific risk exposures fully.

3. **Application Context**: Special form coverage is particularly beneficial in industries where the nature of operations or the value of assets involves high risks or where unpredictable events could cause significant financial setbacks. This includes businesses in areas prone to severe weather conditions, high-value real estate properties, and organizations housing expensive equipment or technology.

4. **Risk Management Strategy**: For insurance professionals, recommending special form coverage is often part of a comprehensive risk management strategy. It involves evaluating the client's specific needs and exposure to potential losses not commonly covered by more basic

policies. By tailoring the insurance package with special form coverage, professionals can provide a robust shield that aligns closely with the risk profile and expectations of the client.

Studying when and how to apply for special form coverage will enable you, my reader, to address the nuanced needs of your clients effectively, ensuring that the coverage provided aligns with the potential risks and challenges the insured faces. This level of customization protects the client's financial interests. It bolsters the trust and reliability perceived in your professional advice and their future insurance agent or broker.

PART III: POLICY APPLICATIONS AND SPECIFIC COVERAGE

Coverage A: Dwelling Coverage Explained

Coverage A, commonly called dwelling coverage, is a fundamental component of homeowners insurance policies. It specifically provides financial protection against physical damage to the home itself due to various covered perils. Understanding the specifics of Coverage A is essential for homeowners to ensure their most valuable asset is adequately protected in the event of a loss.

Dwelling coverage typically includes the structure of the home and any attached features, such as garages, decks, and porches. The coverage is designed to pay for repairs or replacement of the damaged property caused by insured events such as fire, storm damage, vandalism, and other specific perils outlined in the policy. Notably, the level of coverage is determined based on the cost to rebuild the home, not its market value, which can include considerations of the home's size, the materials used in construction, and local construction costs.

It is crucial for homeowners to accurately assess the replacement cost of their home to ensure they purchase sufficient Coverage A limits. Underinsurance can lead to significant financial burdens in the event of major damages where the insurance payout does not cover the entire cost of rebuilding. Additionally, homeowners should be aware of any exclusions or limitations in their policies, such as exclusions for natural disasters like floods or earthquakes, which often require additional coverage.

For insurance professionals, providing clear guidance on accurately calculating the replacement cost and understanding the policyholder's needs and local risks are critical. They should also educate clients on the importance of regularly reviewing and adjusting their coverage to reflect any home improvements, changes in construction costs, or changes in the local real estate market, ensuring that the dwelling coverage continues to meet the homeowner's needs effectively.

Homeowners Policy Types: A Comprehensive Overview

In property insurance, homeowners' policies come in various forms, each tailored to meet different coverage needs and risk profiles. Understanding the nuances of these different policy types is crucial for both insurance professionals and homeowners to ensure that coverage is accurately aligned with the specific requirements and risks of the property owner.

1. **HO-1 (Basic Form)**: This policy offers the most basic level of coverage, protecting against a limited list of perils such as fire, lightning, and explosions. It is less commonly purchased due to its limited scope of protection.

2. **HO-2 (Broad Form)**: This policy provides broader coverage than HO-1 and covers all perils listed in HO-1 plus additional risks like falling objects and damage from the weight of ice, snow, or sleet. It is a named-perils policy, meaning it only covers those risks specifically listed in the policy.

3. **HO-3 (Special Form)**: The most popular among homeowners, this policy offers an open-peril coverage for the structure, meaning it covers all risks except for those explicitly excluded in the policy. Personal property, however, is covered only for named perils.

4. **HO-4 (Contents Broad Form)**: Known as renters insurance, this policy is designed for those who lease their living space. It covers personal property against the same perils as HO-2 and includes liability coverage.

5. **HO-5 (Comprehensive Form)**: Providing the most extensive coverage, this policy offers open-peril coverage for both the structure and personal property, which means it covers all risks except those specifically excluded.

6. **HO-6 (Unit-Owners Form)**: Tailored for condominium owners, this policy covers personal property, liability, and specific parts of the condo unit that the owner is responsible for, as outlined by the association's policy.

7. **HO-8 (Modified Coverage Form)**: Designed for older homes where the replacement cost far exceeds the market value, this policy covers the home for specific perils and often at actual cash value rather than replacement cost.

Each policy type is designed to cater to different living situations and property types, providing a range of coverage levels and premiums. For insurance professionals, offering a comprehensive overview of these options helps clients make informed decisions based on their specific needs, financial goals, and the particular risks associated with their homes. This deep understanding not only aids in tailoring insurance solutions effectively but also in building lasting relationships with clients by ensuring they feel confident and secure in their insurance choices.

Flood Insurance: Coverage Overview and Exclusions

Flood insurance is a specialized property insurance form crucial for homeowners and businesses in flood-prone areas. Unlike standard homeowners policies, which typically exclude flood damage, flood insurance policies are explicitly designed to cover losses caused by flooding, providing financial protection against one of nature's most common and destructive hazards.

1. **Coverage Overview**: Flood insurance generally covers direct physical loss caused by "flood," which is explicitly defined in the policy. This includes inundation from tidal waters, overflow of inland waters, unusual and rapid accumulation or runoff of surface waters, and mudslides. The coverage typically includes the structure of the building and may also cover contents if specified. It compensates for structural damage, including foundation elements, electrical and plumbing systems, central air and heating equipment, and permanently installed cabinets, paneling, and bookcases.

2. **Exclusions**: While flood insurance provides essential coverage, it does have limitations and exclusions. Common exclusions include damage caused by moisture, mildew, or mold that the property owner could have avoided; currency, precious metals, and valuable papers such as stock certificates; outdoor property such as fences, septic systems, and landscaping; and living expenses such as temporary housing.

3. **Mandatory Purchase Requirement**: In areas designated by the Federal Emergency Management Agency (FEMA) as high-risk flood zones, homeowners with mortgages from federally regulated or insured lenders are required to purchase flood insurance. This requirement underscores the importance of flood insurance in protecting against significant financial loss due to flooding.

Earthquake Insurance: Coverage Specifics

Earthquake insurance is a specific type of property insurance designed to cover damage to buildings and personal property resulting from seismic activities. Unlike standard homeowners insurance, which typically excludes earthquake damage, earthquake insurance must be purchased separately to cover this specific risk.

1. **Coverage Overview**: Earthquake insurance policies generally cover damage to the building and personal property within it. This may include major structural damages such as cracked foundations, collapsed walls, and damages to personal belongings inside the home. Policies usually also cover additional living expenses if the home is uninhabitable due to earthquake damage.

2. **Deductibles**: Earthquake insurance policies typically feature high deductibles, which can range from 10% to 20% of the structure's replacement value. This means that the policyholder must

cover a significant portion of the costs before insurance payments kick in, reflecting the high risk and potential high costs associated with earthquake damage.

3. **Exclusions and Limitations**: Common exclusions in earthquake insurance include damage to vehicles, land (such as landscaping, pools, fences), and government-imposed repairs or upgrades. Policies might also limit coverage for certain types of personal property and require specific retrofitting measures to qualify for coverage.

4. **Regional Considerations**: The necessity and cost of earthquake insurance can vary significantly depending on the geographic area. In regions with high seismic activity, such as California, earthquake insurance is more common and can be crucial for financial protection against potential losses.

By accurately assessing the need for earthquake insurance based on location and potential risk, insurance professionals can provide valuable guidance to clients, ensuring they are adequately protected against the devastating impacts of earthquakes. This expertise goes beyond mere transactional advice—it builds a foundation of trust and reliability between the client and the insurance provider, enhancing the long-term resilience of communities in earthquake-prone areas.

Personal Auto Insurance: Key Coverage Areas

Personal auto insurance is a mandatory requirement for vehicle owners and provides comprehensive financial protection in various situations involving vehicles. The policy encompasses several key coverage areas, which include:

1. **Liability Coverage**: This is the most fundamental aspect of auto insurance, required by law in most states. It covers the costs associated with injuries and property damage the policyholder is responsible for in the event of an accident. This includes bodily injury liability, which pays for medical expenses, lost wages, and other associated costs of injuries to others, and property damage liability, which covers repairing or replacing damaged property.

2. **Collision Coverage**: This covers damage to the policyholder's vehicle resulting from a collision with another vehicle or object, regardless of who is at fault. Collision coverage is crucial for repairing or replacing a damaged vehicle and is typically required if the vehicle is financed or leased.

3. **Comprehensive Coverage**: Also known as "other than collision" coverage, this protects against theft, vandalism, natural disasters, and other damages not resulting from a collision. It helps ensure the vehicle owner can repair or replace the vehicle in situations such as fire, hail, or falling objects.

4. **Uninsured/Underinsured Motorist Coverage**: This provides protection when the policyholder is involved in an accident with a driver who either lacks sufficient insurance or

insurance. It can cover both bodily injuries and property damage, offering crucial financial protection in accidents where the at-fault driver cannot cover the losses.

5. **Medical Payments/Personal Injury Protection (PIP)**: This coverage pays for medical treatment of the driver and passengers of the policyholder's car in the event of an accident. PIP can also cover other expenses such as rehabilitation services, funeral costs, and lost wages.

Umbrella Policies: Extended Liability Coverage

Umbrella insurance is a form of liability insurance that provides an additional layer of security beyond existing limits and coverages of other policies, such as auto or homeowners insurance. It is particularly valuable in protecting against large and potentially devastating liability claims or judgments.

1. **Broad Coverage**: Umbrella policies kick in when the limits of the underlying liability coverage are reached. They cover a broader array of scenarios, potentially including libel, slander, false arrest, and liability coverage on rental units the insured might own.

2. **High Coverage Limits**: Typically, umbrella policies start with $1 million in coverage and can go much higher. This high limit is beneficial in protecting assets against large lawsuits that could otherwise financially devastate an individual or family.

3. **Cost-Effective Protection**: Given the high coverage limits, umbrella policies are generally cost-effective, providing substantial additional coverage for a relatively low additional premium. This cost-effectiveness makes it an attractive option for increasing liability coverage without significantly increasing insurance costs.

4. **Coverage for Legal Fees**: In addition to covering damages, umbrella policies also cover legal fees and other expenses related to lawsuits, further protecting the insured's financial stability.

PART IV: RISK MANAGEMENT, PREMIUMS AND UNDERWRITING

Underwriting Process in Property and Casualty Insurance

The underwriting process is a fundamental aspect of property and casualty insurance, involving the systematic evaluation of risks associated with insuring people and property. Underwriters assess these risks to determine the terms and conditions of insurance coverage, ultimately deciding whether to insure the risk and at what premium rate.

1. Risk Evaluation: Underwriters start by collecting and analyzing data on potential clients to assess the level of risk. This data can include information on the property's location, construction materials, age, and protective measures (like security systems and fire suppressants).

2. Rating and Pricing: Based on the risk assessment, underwriters apply actuarial data to set pricing for premiums. They consider loss history, potential maximum loss, replacement costs, and other actuarial considerations to arrive at a balanced rate that protects the insurer while offering value to the insured.

3. Policy Issuance: Underwriters prepare and issue the insurance policy after determining the premium and policy terms. This stage may involve additional negotiations and adjustments based on feedback from the potential policyholder or their agents.

The underwriting process not only determines who gets insured and at what cost but also plays a critical role in maintaining the financial health of insurance companies. Effective underwriting ensures that the risks taken are calculated and the premiums collected are adequate to cover losses, thereby securing the company's long-term viability.

Risk Assessment Techniques for Property and Casualty Insurance

Property and casualty insurance risk assessment is critical to determining how much coverage the insured should receive and at what cost. This process involves identifying the potential risks associated with insuring a property or individual and quantifying the likely impact of those risks.

1. Identification of Risks: This initial step involves understanding all potential risks that could cause loss or damage. Property insurance might include natural disasters, theft, or fire. For casualty insurance, it could involve assessing the likelihood of legal liability for injuries or other damages.

2. Quantitative and Qualitative Assessments: Insurers use quantitative methods (like statistical analysis and probability models) and qualitative assessments (such as historical data and industry trends) to gauge the frequency and severity of these risks.

3. Mitigation Strategies: Part of risk assessment is recommending ways to mitigate risks. This might involve suggesting improvements to physical security, better compliance practices, or changes in operational procedures to reduce claims' likelihood or potential impact.

Understanding and implementing advanced risk assessment techniques allow insurers to more accurately price premiums and design coverage that reflects the true nature of the risk, thereby protecting both the insurer's and the insured's interests.

Premium Calculation and Factors Affecting Rates

Calculating premiums in property and casualty insurance is a complex process influenced by many factors determining the cost of providing coverage. Understanding these factors is crucial for insurance professionals to price policies effectively and for consumers to understand their insurance costs.

1. Risk Exposure: The greater the risk of a claim, the higher the premium. This is determined based on factors such as the property's location, its use, the claim history of the area or individual, and the physical condition of the property.

2. Coverage Amount: The amount of coverage requested also impacts the premium. Higher coverage limits increase the insurer's potential liability in case of a claim, thereby increasing the premium.

3. Deductibles and Policy Terms: Higher deductibles generally lower premiums because the insured assumes more risk. Similarly, the specific terms and conditions of the policy, such as exclusions and endorsements, can also affect the premium.

4. External Factors: Economic inflation, legal trends, and technological advancements influence premium levels. For instance, increased costs in building materials will affect the premiums for property insurance.

By considering all these factors, insurers can set equitable premiums for the insured while ensuring that the insurance company remains financially sound to cover all potential claims. This balance is critical to the ongoing sustainability of the insurance market.

Coinsurance in Property Insurance: Importance and Calculation Examples

Coinsurance is a crucial concept in property insurance that affects both policy coverage and premium costs. It is a clause typically included in commercial and sometimes residential property insurance policies that require the insured to carry a minimum amount of insurance relative to the property's value.

1. **Purpose of Coinsurance**: The primary purpose of coinsurance is to encourage policyholders to insure their property to a value close to its actual replacement cost. It helps prevent underinsurance, a significant risk for insurance companies if many policyholders under-report values to lower their premiums.

2. **Calculation of Coinsurance**: Coinsurance is typically expressed as a percentage (commonly 80%, 90%, or 100%) of the total value of the insured property that the policyholder must maintain as insurance coverage. Suppose a claim occurs, and it is found that the amount of coverage is less than the coinsurance percentage of the actual replacement value. In that case, the claim payment may be reduced. The formula used is (Amount of Insurance Carried / Amount of Insurance Required) x Loss = Claim Payment.

3. **Example**: For instance, if a building valued at $100,000 has a coinsurance requirement of 90%, the policyholder should have at least $90,000 in coverage. If only $80,000 in coverage is purchased and a $20,000 loss occurs, the insurer would only pay ($80,000 / $90,000) x $20,000 = $17,777.78.

Pro Rata Cancellation of Insurance: Calculation and Examples

Pro rata cancellation of an insurance policy is when the insurer cancels the policy before its expiration date and refunds the remaining premium to the insured based on the exact number of days the policy was in effect. This method is one of the fairest ways of calculating the return premium.

1. **Application of Pro Rata Cancellation**: This cancellation method is typically used when the policyholder decides to cancel the policy and has not violated any policy conditions. It ensures that the policyholder only pays for the coverage they have used.

2. **Calculation**: The formula for pro rata cancellation is: (Unearned Premium / Total Premium) x Number of Days Policy was in Force = Return Premium.

3. **Example**: If a policyholder has a 12-month insurance policy costing $1,200 and decides to cancel after three months, the return premium would be calculated as follows: ($1,200 / 12 months) x 9 remaining months = $900 returned to the policyholder.

Insurance professionals need to be adept at explaining and calculating pro-rata cancellations, ensuring clients understand how changes in their coverage might financially impact them. This transparency helps maintain trust and satisfaction among clients.

Short Rate Cancellation: Understanding the Penalties and Calculations

Short-rate cancellation is another method of calculating the return premium when a policy is canceled before its expiration date. Unlike pro rata cancellation, short rate cancellation includes a penalty that the insured must pay, compensating the insurer for the administrative costs of maintaining and terminating the policy early.

1. **Purpose and Application**: This method is used primarily when the policyholder initiates the cancellation. The penalty is meant to dissuade policyholders from canceling their policies prematurely unless necessary.

2. **Calculation**: The formula for a short-rate cancellation usually involves a table that determines the penalty percentage based on how much of the policy term has elapsed. The return premium is then calculated by subtracting the penalty from the unearned premium.

3. **Example**: Using the same 12-month, $1,200 policy — if the policyholder cancels after three months and the short rate penalty is 10% of the unearned premium, the calculation would be: $900 (unearned premium) - $90 (penalty) = $810 returned to the policyholder.

Actual Cash Value (ACV) vs. Replacement Cost: Key Differences

Understanding the distinction between Actual Cash Value (ACV) and Replacement Cost is vital in property insurance, as it significantly affects how claims are settled following property damage or loss.

1. **Actual Cash Value**: ACV is a valuation method that considers the depreciation of the property. It is calculated by taking the replacement cost of an item and subtracting depreciation due to age, wear and tear, or obsolescence. This method results in lower payouts because it reflects the item's current market value, not what it would cost to buy new.

2. **Replacement Cost**: Unlike ACV, replacement cost coverage reimburses the policyholder without accounting for depreciation. This coverage pays the cost of replacing the damaged or lost property with new, similar items at current market prices. It ensures that the policyholder can return to a similar position before the loss without considering the depreciated value of the items.

3. **Implications for Policyholders**: The choice between ACV and replacement cost can significantly affect premiums and claim settlements. Policies with replacement cost coverage

generally have higher premiums because they potentially lead to larger claim payouts. Policyholders need to assess their ability to bear out-of-pocket costs when choosing between ACV and replacement cost, considering factors like the age and condition of their property.

Loss Settlement Options: Replacement Cost vs. Actual Cash Value

Loss settlement options in insurance policies dictate how claims are assessed and paid, impacting the financial outcome for the policyholder after a loss. Understanding the nuances between Replacement Cost and Actual Cash Value settlement options is crucial.

1. **Replacement Cost Settlement**: This option allows the policyholder to repair or replace the damaged property without a deduction for depreciation. It provides the insured with sufficient funds to replace the lost or damaged item with a new one of similar kind and quality, subject to policy limits.

2. **Actual Cash Value Settlement**: This approach provides compensation based on the replacement cost minus depreciation. It reflects the item's fair market value at the time of the loss, which may not be adequate to cover the cost of purchasing a new item equivalent to the lost or damaged one.

3. **Choosing Between the Two**: The choice between these settlement options affects the insurance premiums and the extent of coverage. Replacement cost policies are more expensive but offer more comprehensive coverage, making them suitable for newer or well-maintained properties. ACV policies are less costly but may leave the policyholder with additional out-of-pocket expenses in the event of a claim.

Reinsurance: Principles and Practices

Reinsurance is an insurance practice where insurance companies purchase their own insurance policies from other insurers to reduce the risk associated with underwritten policies. This practice is critical to maintaining industry stability and managing large-scale risks.

1. **Purpose of Reinsurance**: The primary goal is to protect insurers by spreading the risks of underwritten policies across multiple parties. This protection becomes crucial in events involving significant losses, such as natural disasters or large-scale liability claims, which could be financially devastating for a single insurer.

2. **Types of Reinsurance**: There are two main types of reinsurance:

   - **Treaty Reinsurance**: Automatic coverage for a portion of an insurer's portfolio, negotiated in advance.

- **Facultative Reinsurance**: Coverage tailored for specific, individual risks not covered under treaty reinsurance agreements.

3. **Benefits of Reinsurance**: Beyond risk mitigation, reinsurance allows insurers to increase their underwriting capacity, stabilize financial performance, and improve capital management. It enables insurers to accept larger policies or a greater volume of policies than they could safely handle alone.

Reinsurance is a complex but indispensable aspect of the insurance industry, ensuring that insurers can continue to offer substantial coverage options without exposing themselves to unsustainable risks. Insurance professionals must understand these principles to effectively manage risks and maintain the financial health of their insurance operations.

Bonds: Surety and Fidelity

Bonds, specifically surety and fidelity bonds, play an essential role in the insurance and financial sectors by guaranteeing performance or assurance against financial loss due to dishonest acts.

1. **Surety Bonds**: These are designed to meet contractual and legal obligations. A surety bond involves three parties: the principal (who needs the bond), the obligee (to whom the bond is given as a guarantee), and the surety (the insurance company guaranteeing the principal's obligation). Surety bonds are commonly used in the construction industry to ensure that contractors complete projects as agreed or in businesses where fidelity to perform duties as agreed is crucial.

2. **Fidelity Bonds**: Also known as fidelity insurance, these bonds protect businesses from losses caused by fraudulent acts committed by specified employees. These bonds cover financial loss due to employee theft, embezzlement, or forgery. Fidelity bonds are essential in industries where employees handle cash or valuable assets.

3. **Applications and Benefits**: Both types of bonds provide a critical layer of security that enhances trust in business transactions and employment practices. They help companies manage risk by providing financial compensation in cases of non-compliance with terms or dishonest activities, thereby safeguarding the company's assets and reputation.

Insurance professionals must understand the nuances of surety and fidelity bonds, as they advise businesses on risk management strategies and appropriate coverage options to protect against specific liabilities and potential financial losses.

PART V: LEGAL FRAMEWORK, CLAIMS, AND REGULATIONS

Insurance Regulations and Laws

Insurance regulations and laws are foundational to the functioning of the insurance industry, ensuring that operations are conducted fairly, transparently, and financially soundly.

1. **Regulatory Framework**: Insurance is regulated primarily at the state level in the United States, with each state having its own set of laws and regulatory bodies, typically led by a state insurance commissioner. These regulations govern licensing, solvency requirements, rate approvals, policy forms, and consumer protections.

2. **Key Legislation**: Several critical pieces of legislation have shaped the insurance industry. These include laws like the McCarran-Ferguson Act, which gives states the authority to regulate insurance, and the Health Insurance Portability and Accountability Act (HIPAA), which impacts how personal health information is handled.

3. **Compliance Requirements**: Insurers must adhere to complex regulatory requirements, including financial reporting standards, market conduct examinations, and consumer data protection laws. Compliance ensures the financial health of the insurance companies and protects policyholders from unfair practices.

For insurance professionals, a thorough understanding of insurance regulations and laws is about compliance and navigating the legal landscape effectively. This knowledge allows them to better serve their clients by ensuring that all activities are within the bounds of the law and by advocating for their clients' rights under the policy and the law.

State-Specific Insurance Regulations and Laws

Understanding the nuances of state-specific insurance regulations and laws is crucial for anyone entering the insurance industry, as insurance is regulated primarily at the state level within the United States. Each state has its own regulatory framework, which includes variations in licensing requirements, consumer protection laws, and specific mandates for insurance coverage. However, despite these variations, this book's fundamental principles and concepts are universally applicable across all states, providing a solid foundation for understanding any local regulations.

1. **Regulatory Authorities**: Each state operates under its own Department of Insurance, overseen by an Insurance Commissioner. These bodies enforce local insurance laws and oversee all insurance-related activities within the state. They ensure that companies and professionals adhere to financial solvency, ethical practices, and consumer protection standards.

2. **Licensing and Education**: While specific licensing requirements can vary, the core knowledge and competencies required to obtain a license are consistent nationwide. This book covers these essential topics, preparing you to meet state-specific requirements and giving you a comprehensive overview that applies universally.

3. **Product and Rate Regulation**: States individually review and approve insurance products and rates, but the criteria for evaluation—such as fairness, adequacy, and non-discrimination—are common across different jurisdictions. Understanding these basic evaluation principles will prepare you to navigate and comply with various state regulations effectively.

4. **Consumer Protection Laws**: Although the specifics can vary, the purpose of state consumer protection laws is consistent: to ensure fair treatment of policyholders and provide precise mechanisms for claims and disputes. The principles governing these laws are similar nationwide, focusing on transparency, fairness, and the rights of policyholders.

5. **Market Conduct and Compliance**: Each state monitors the marketing and sale of insurance products to prevent deceptive practices. However, the ethical guidelines and professional standards discussed in this book are designed to help you understand and adhere to the highest standards of conduct, regardless of state-specific rules.

6. **Adapting to Local Needs**: This book also provides strategies for adapting to the specific insurance landscape of different states, helping you apply the fundamental concepts learned to meet local requirements effectively.

While state-specific regulations may dictate the finer points of practice and procedure, the foundational knowledge provided in this book arms you with the essential principles needed to operate effectively in any state. This ensures that regardless of where you choose to practice, you are well-prepared to navigate the complexities of the U.S. insurance regulatory environment, enhancing your professionalism and credibility in the field.

Overview of Key State-Specific Insurance Regulations

In this chapter, we focus on the insurance laws and regulations of the ten U.S. states with the most significant demand for insurance examinations and services. These states have been selected due to their large populations, high economic activity, and unique environmental factors influencing insurance needs and regulatory responses. Here is a brief overview of each state and the reason for its inclusion:

1. California

Selected for its rigorous consumer protection laws and unique earthquake insurance requirements, reflecting its high seismic activity.

2. Texas

Notable for its specific windstorm insurance regulations, crucial due to the state's susceptibility to hurricanes and severe storms.

3. Florida

Included for its stringent hurricane and flood insurance mandates, essential in a state frequently affected by tropical storms and flooding.

4. New York

Chosen for its complex life and health insurance regulations and aggressive stance on cybersecurity for insurance companies.

5. Illinois

Recognized for its strong consumer protections in health insurance and a comprehensive approach to insurance education and transparency.

6. Georgia

Highlighted for its high minimum auto insurance coverage requirements and detailed rules on post-accident claims processes.

7. Pennsylvania

Focuses on workers' compensation insurance, with specific incentives for businesses that adhere to state safety guidelines.

8. Ohio

Selected for its emphasis on transparency in policy terms and conditions, especially in life and annuity products.

9. Michigan

Known for recent reforms in auto insurance, particularly regarding personal injury protection (PIP) and the impact on premium costs.

10. North Carolina

Included for its unique method of calculating homeowners insurance premiums based on geographical and meteorological data, and specific life insurance consumer protections.

Each of these states presents distinct challenges and opportunities in the insurance sector, necessitating a deep understanding of their specific regulatory landscapes. This knowledge is crucial for compliance and for providing tailored and effective insurance solutions to meet the diverse needs of clients in these regions. Let's now delve into each point to provide a deeper understanding of the insurance regulatory environment in each state.

Navigating California's Unique Insurance Landscape: A Deep Dive into State-Specific Laws

California, known for its dynamic economy and diverse natural landscapes, also possesses one of the most complex regulatory environments in the United States, particularly in the insurance field. The state's unique geographical features and high propensity for natural disasters such as earthquakes and wildfires have shaped its distinctive insurance laws and regulations. This article explores the nuances of California's insurance landscape, focusing on consumer protection, earthquake insurance mandates, and wildfire coverage, highlighting the challenges and considerations for insurance professionals operating within the state.

Consumer Protection at the Forefront

California's approach to insurance regulation is heavily weighted towards consumer protection. The California Department of Insurance (CDI), led by the Insurance Commissioner, is proactive in ensuring that insurance policies are fair, transparent, and comprehensively protect the state's residents. Proposition 103, passed in 1988, is a significant piece of legislation that requires prior approval of property and casualty rates before they can be applied. This proposition also mandates that insurers justify rate changes, proving them necessary and fair. This regulatory framework ensures that consumers are not subjected to arbitrary rate increases and that any rate adjustments are warranted in the context of coverage offered.

Earthquake Insurance: A State-Specific Staple

Given California's high seismic risk, earthquake insurance regulations are particularly stringent. Unlike most other states, where earthquake coverage might be an optional addition to homeowners' policies, California has established the California Earthquake Authority (CEA) to provide basic earthquake coverage. Participation in the CEA by insurers is voluntary, but those who do not participate must offer their earthquake policies, which has led to a well-developed market for this coverage. The policies usually cover structural damage to the home, loss of personal possessions, and additional living expenses if the home is uninhabitable. However, these policies often come with high deductibles, reflecting the significant risk of seismic activity.

Wildfire Coverage and the FAIR Plan

Wildfires are another critical concern in California's insurance landscape. In response to the increasing frequency and severity of wildfires, California has adapted its insurance regulations to manage wildfire risks better. Insurers must consider and implement fire-hardening improvements when they renew or write new policies for properties in wildfire-prone areas. Moreover, the California FAIR Plan, a state-mandated "insurer of last resort," provides basic fire insurance coverage for homeowners who cannot obtain insurance in the private market due to their property's wildfire risk. This plan ensures that residents in high-risk areas are not left uninsured against potential losses due to wildfires.

Challenges for Insurance Professionals

For insurance professionals, navigating California's regulatory environment requires a deep understanding of both the broad principles of insurance law and the specific provisions applicable to the state. Professionals must stay informed about ongoing legislative changes, such as those related to climate change and natural disasters, which could further affect insurance practices and policies. The state's emphasis on consumer rights and protections also necessitates that insurers maintain high standards of transparency and fairness in all their dealings.

California's insurance laws exemplify the state's commitment to protecting its citizens from the financial risks of natural disasters while balancing the need for a stable and sustainable insurance market. For insurance professionals, operating in California offers both challenges and opportunities to innovate in product offerings and risk management strategies. By understanding and adhering to state-specific regulations, insurance providers can comply with the law and significantly contribute to the safety and stability of the communities they serve. The complexity of California's insurance landscape also underscores the importance of ongoing education and adaptation in the face of evolving environmental and regulatory conditions.

Texas Insurance Regulations: Tailored Strategies in a State Prone to Natural Disasters

Texas stands as a behemoth in the insurance industry, not just because of its size and economic prowess but also due to the variety of natural disasters it faces, from hurricanes and floods to tornadoes and hailstorms. These environmental challenges have shaped a distinctive regulatory framework that is crucial for insurance professionals to understand. This article delves into the specifics of Texas's insurance landscape, emphasizing windstorm coverage, the Texas Windstorm Insurance Association (TWIA), and flood insurance considerations, providing a comprehensive overview for industry professionals.

Emphasis on Windstorm and Hail Coverage

The need for specialized windstorm and hail insurance in Texas is particularly acute due to the state's susceptibility to hurricanes along the Gulf Coast. Standard homeowners' policies in Texas typically do not cover damage from these perils unless specifically added, which led to the establishment of the Texas Windstorm Insurance Association (TWIA). TWIA acts as a last resort insurer, offering windstorm and hail insurance to residents of Texas's 14 coastal counties and parts of Harris County, who cannot obtain this coverage in the private market.

Understanding the Texas Windstorm Insurance Association

The TWIA was created by the Texas Legislature in 1971 in response to Hurricane Celia and provides crucial windstorm and hail coverage. It ensures that coastal residents, particularly those in high-risk areas, have access to necessary insurance to cover potential losses from severe wind and hail events. Coverage through TWIA is contingent on properties meeting specific building codes designed to enhance their resilience against wind damage. The association regularly updates these requirements to reflect new construction and disaster resilience standards.

For insurance professionals, understanding and communicating the requirements and benefits of TWIA coverage to potential clients is essential. They must navigate the application process, ensure properties comply with TWIA standards, and help policyholders understand the scope of coverage and the importance of regular updates to reflect property improvements and market changes.

Flood Insurance Considerations

Apart from wind-related events, flooding is a significant risk in Texas, especially in low-lying and coastal areas. Unlike some other states, Texas does not have a state-managed flood insurance program, and coverage is primarily obtained through the National Flood Insurance Program (NFIP). Following significant flooding events, such as those caused by Hurricane Harvey, there has been increased attention on the adequacy of flood maps and the need for updated risk assessments.

Texas insurance professionals need to be adept at navigating the NFIP, understanding its coverage limitations, and advising clients on supplemental policies when necessary. This includes assessing whether a client's area is correctly mapped, understanding the implications of being in or out of a designated flood zone, and helping clients manage the cost of flood insurance, which can fluctuate based on new data and changing environmental conditions.

Regulatory and Legislative Landscape

The Texas Department of Insurance (TDI) regulates the state's insurance industry, ensuring that companies remain solvent, policies are fair, and consumers are protected. Texas's legislative environment is dynamic, with regular sessions that may introduce changes affecting coverage requirements, consumer rights, and the regulatory powers of the TDI. For professionals in the insurance sector, staying informed about legislative developments is critical. It ensures compliance and enables them to provide their clients with the most current and relevant advice.

Operating in the Texas insurance market requires a thorough understanding of both the unique environmental risks and the specific regulatory responses tailored to address these challenges. For insurance professionals, mastering the details of windstorm and flood insurance, and keeping abreast of legislative changes, are paramount tasks. This knowledge not only aids in offering clients better services but also enhances their ability to adapt to an ever-evolving market landscape. As Texas continues to grow and face new challenges, the role of informed and proactive insurance professionals has never been more critical in helping to protect its residents and businesses.

Navigating Florida's Unique Insurance Environment: Focus on Hurricane and Flood Coverage

Florida's insurance landscape is notably shaped by its geographical susceptibility to hurricanes and floods, making its regulatory framework particularly complex and dynamic. Given the state's history of devastating hurricanes and the ongoing challenges related to flood management, understanding Florida's specific insurance requirements and policies is essential for professionals operating within this high-risk environment.

Hurricane Insurance Requirements

In Florida, hurricane coverage is generally included as part of a standard homeowner's insurance policy, but the specifics of this coverage can vary significantly based on the insurer and the policy details. After the extensive damage caused by hurricanes like Andrew and Irma, Florida has implemented stringent building codes to strengthen properties against hurricane damage, influencing insurance practices and premiums.

1. Deductibles for Hurricane Damage: Florida law allows insurance companies to require a separate hurricane deductible, which is typically a percentage of the policy limits. This deductible applies specifically to damage caused by hurricanes, as officially declared by the National Weather Service, and can range from 1% to 5% of the home's insured value, depending on the policy terms and the property's location.

2. Rate Filings: Insurers in Florida must submit their rate filings to the Florida Office of Insurance Regulation, which reviews and approves these rates. The process ensures that rates are not excessive yet adequate to cover potential losses, especially in high-risk areas.

Flood Insurance Dynamics

Despite being surrounded by water and frequently experiencing heavy rains, flood coverage is not included in standard homeowners policies in Florida. It must be purchased separately, usually through the National Flood Insurance Program (NFIP). Given the flat terrain and the prevalence of coastal properties, a significant portion of Florida's population lives in flood-prone areas, making flood insurance a critical consideration.

1. Flood Insurance Requirements: Purchasing flood insurance is mandatory for homeowners with mortgages from federally backed lenders and living in high-risk flood zones. However, recent years have seen efforts to encourage even those outside designated high-risk areas to obtain flood insurance, reflecting broader environmental changes and increased rainfall levels.

2. Private Flood Insurance: Besides the NFIP, Florida has been at the forefront of encouraging the development of private flood insurance markets. This initiative aims to provide more options to consumers, potentially lower insurance costs, and foster a more competitive insurance market.

Regulatory and Consumer Protection Efforts

The Florida Department of Financial Services, along with the Office of Insurance Regulation, actively works to protect consumers through various initiatives. These include improving the transparency of insurance practices, ensuring fair and timely claims processing, especially after major hurricanes, and promoting financial literacy regarding the importance of adequate insurance coverage.

1. Claims Handling Regulations: Florida has specific regulations designed to expedite the claims process following a hurricane. Insurers must handle claims promptly, with deadlines for acknowledging claims, starting investigations, and making payments.

2. Mitigation Discounts: Florida law mandates that insurers offer discounts or credits for homes with wind mitigation features that exceed state building codes. These features significantly reduce the risk of damage and subsequent claims, which is reflected in lower premiums for homeowners.

For insurance professionals, operating in Florida requires a thorough understanding of specific local insurance requirements and a proactive approach to staying informed about regulatory changes and market developments. The unique challenges posed by Florida's environment necessitate an adept handling of both hurricane and flood insurance, ensuring that clients are well-protected against the state's natural disaster risks. This expertise is crucial not only for compliance but also for providing effective and comprehensive insurance solutions tailored to the specific needs of Florida residents.

Mastering New York's Insurance Regulatory Landscape: A Focus on Life and Cybersecurity Regulations

New York's insurance sector is marked by its rigorous regulatory environment, especially in life insurance and cybersecurity areas. As one of the world's financial capitals, the state imposes stringent requirements to ensure that the insurance industry operates transparently and remains resilient against various risks, including cyber threats.

Life Insurance Regulations in New York

New York is known for its comprehensive and consumer-oriented approach to life insurance regulation. The state's policies ensure maximum transparency and fairness, providing robust protection for policyholders.

1. Disclosure Requirements: New York mandates detailed disclosure during the life insurance sales process, ensuring that consumers are fully informed about the terms and costs of policies. Insurers must provide applicants with clear, understandable information about any life insurance policy's benefits, limitations, and costs before purchase.

2. External Review Process: New York requires that life insurance companies submit their policy forms for approval before they can be sold. This review process ensures that policies comply with state laws and regulations concerning fairness and adequacy of coverage terms.

3. Consumer Protections: The state offers solid protections for life insurance policyholders, including grace periods for late payments, rights to appeal against denied claims, and guarantees against unfair discrimination in underwriting and pricing.

Cybersecurity Regulations

Given the significant presence of financial services industries in New York, the state has established itself as a leader in developing regulations to protect sensitive consumer information against cyber threats.

1. Cybersecurity Requirements: The New York Department of Financial Services (NYDFS) has implemented one of the nation's first cybersecurity regulations for financial service companies, including insurers. These regulations require companies to assess their risk profiles and design a cybersecurity program that effectively addresses those risks.

2. Cybersecurity Policy Elements: Insurers must appoint a Chief Information Security Officer, conduct periodic risk assessments, maintain a cybersecurity program designed to protect the confidentiality, integrity, and availability of information systems, and implement controls and plans to ensure the safety and soundness of the institution.

3. Reporting Obligations: Firms are required to report cybersecurity events to regulatory bodies within 72 hours of discovery, significantly if the event impacts the firm's operations or involves actual or potentially harmful unauthorized access to information.

Regulatory Bodies and Compliance

The New York State Department of Financial Services (DFS) oversees the operation of insurance companies in the state, ensuring they adhere to the laws and regulations. Compliance is rigorously enforced through regular audits, inspections, and penalties for non-compliance.

1. Market Conduct Examinations: These examinations assess how well insurers comply with state regulations in their day-to-day operations. They cover aspects such as the treatment of policyholders, the accuracy of contract language, and the timeliness of claim payments.

2. Financial Health Audits: New York regulators frequently audit the financial health of insurance companies to prevent insolvency. These audits help ensure that insurers have sufficient reserves to pay future claims and are solvent enough to withstand market fluctuations.

For insurance professionals, operating in New York requires meticulous adherence to a complex set of regulations that cover every aspect of the insurance business, from product offerings and sales practices to claims management and corporate governance. Understanding and navigating these regulations is crucial for maintaining compliance and delivering the best possible service to consumers in New York.

The state's proactive stance on issues like life insurance transparency and cybersecurity sets a high standard for the industry, promoting trust and stability in one of the world's most significant insurance markets.

Illinois: A Model of Consumer Protection and Insurance Regulation

Illinois is recognized for its robust insurance regulation framework that emphasizes consumer protection, particularly in health insurance and general insurance practices. The state's regulations ensure that insurance policies are sold and managed in a fair and beneficial way to consumers. This section delves into the specifics of Illinois' insurance landscape, focusing on its consumer-friendly laws, the regulatory environment, and the efforts to ensure transparency and fairness in the insurance market.

Health Insurance Regulations

Illinois places a strong emphasis on protecting consumers in the health insurance sector. This includes comprehensive regulations around coverage requirements and the rights of policyholders.

1. Mental Health Parity: Illinois has strict laws requiring health insurance plans to offer coverage for mental health and substance use disorders that is on par with coverage for physical health conditions. This ensures that individuals have access to necessary mental health services without facing higher costs or fewer benefits than those applicable to physical health conditions.

2. Pre-existing Conditions: Following federal guidelines, Illinois mandates that health insurance providers cannot refuse coverage or charge higher premiums based on pre-existing conditions. This regulation is crucial for ensuring all individuals have access to necessary health care services without discrimination.

3. Marketplace Accessibility: Illinois operates a state-partnered health insurance marketplace under the Affordable Care Act, providing an accessible platform for residents to compare and purchase health insurance plans. This marketplace also offers subsidies to make health insurance more affordable for low and middle-income families.

Consumer Protections in General Insurance

Beyond health insurance, Illinois has developed a series of laws and regulations that safeguard consumers across various types of insurance policies, focusing on transparency and fair treatment.

1. Cancellation and Renewal: Illinois law provides clear rules regarding canceling and renewing insurance policies. Insurers must give adequate notice before canceling or not renewing a policy and explain the reasons for their decision. This transparency helps consumers understand their rights and the steps they can take to contest a decision or find alternative coverage.

2. Claims Processing: Regulations require insurers to handle claims promptly and fairly. If a claim is denied, the insurer must clearly explain the reasons for the denial. Policyholders have the right

to appeal denied claims, a process that the Illinois Department of Insurance oversees to ensure fairness.

3. Consumer Complaints: The Illinois Department of Insurance offers a well-structured system for handling consumer complaints against insurance companies. This system ensures that consumer grievances regarding unfair practices or disputes over claims are addressed properly, helping to maintain trust in the insurance system.

Regulatory Oversight

The Illinois Department of Insurance actively monitors the insurance industry to ensure state laws and regulations compliance. This oversight is critical for maintaining the integrity of the insurance market.

1. Regular Audits: Illinois insurance companies are subject to regular audits to ensure they have the financial stability to meet their obligations to policyholders and comply with state insurance laws.

2. License Regulation: The state rigorously regulates the licensing of insurance agents and companies, ensuring that only qualified individuals and entities offer insurance services. This includes requirements for ongoing education and ethical standards.

For insurance professionals working in Illinois, a deep understanding of the state's consumer protection laws and regulatory requirements is essential. Illinois' approach to insurance regulation prioritizes consumers' rights and well-being and supports a stable and trustworthy insurance market. By adhering to these regulations, insurance providers can better serve their clients and contribute positively to the broader community.

Georgia's Insurance Landscape: Balancing Robust Consumer Protections with Industry Growth

Georgia's insurance sector is characterized by its balanced approach to regulation, ensuring robust consumer protections while fostering a competitive market environment.

Auto Insurance Regulations in Georgia

Auto insurance is a critical area of focus in Georgia, given the state's heavy reliance on motor vehicles for transportation across its sprawling urban and rural areas.

1. Minimum Coverage Requirements: Georgia mandates that all drivers carry auto liability insurance. The required minimum limits are higher than many other states, set at $25,000 for bodily injury per person, $50,000 for bodily injury per accident, and $25,000 for property damage per accident. These limits ensure adequate financial protection against the costs associated with accidents.

2. Uninsured Motorist Coverage: While not mandatory, Georgia strongly encourages drivers to carry coverage for uninsured motorists (UM) and underinsured motorists (UIM). This additional coverage protects drivers in the event of an accident where the other party does not have sufficient insurance to cover the damages.

3. No-Fault System: Georgia operates under a traditional tort system rather than a no-fault system, meaning that the driver who is legally responsible for an accident and their insurance will pay for the other party's medical expenses, vehicle repairs, and other costs stemming from the accident.

Health Insurance Oversight

Georgia's approach to health insurance is also noteworthy, particularly in its management of the Affordable Care Act (ACA) provisions and state-specific health initiatives.

1. ACA Implementation: Georgia has opted to use the federally facilitated marketplace for health insurance, which allows residents to access various plan options and apply for federal subsidies to help cover the cost of premiums.

2. Medicaid and State-Sponsored Programs: While Georgia has been conservative in its approach to Medicaid expansion, the state offers several programs aimed at providing coverage for children, pregnant women, and certain low-income adults. These programs are critical in reducing the uninsured rate and providing necessary health services.

3. Mental Health Coverage: Following broader trends, Georgia requires that insurance policies include coverage for mental health conditions, ensuring parity with physical health conditions. This mandate helps address the growing recognition of mental health's critical role in overall well-being.

Regulatory Framework and Consumer Protections

The Georgia Department of Insurance (GDI) plays a pivotal role in regulating the state's insurance market, ensuring that the industry operates fairly and transparently.

1. Consumer Services Division: The GDI's Consumer Services Division is particularly active, offering assistance to Georgians in understanding their insurance policies, filing complaints, and resolving disputes with insurers. This division is an essential resource for ensuring consumer rights are upheld.

2. Market Conduct Examinations: Georgia conducts regular examinations of insurance providers to ensure compliance with state laws and regulations. These examinations help maintain high standards within the industry, promoting consumer confidence and ensuring that companies are financially robust and operate ethically.

3. Education and Outreach: The GDI also focuses on educating consumers about their insurance options and rights. This proactive approach helps Georgians make informed decisions about their insurance needs and fosters a more transparent and service-oriented marketplace.

Navigating the insurance landscape in Georgia requires a thorough understanding of the specific regulations and the broader regulatory environment. For insurance professionals, staying informed about Georgia's evolving laws and policies is crucial for providing accurate advice and effective client services. Georgia's balanced approach to insurance regulation protects consumers and supports a healthy, competitive market that benefits providers and policyholders alike.

Pennsylvania: Emphasizing Worker Protections and Market Stability

Pennsylvania's insurance sector is characterized by its strong protections for workers through comprehensive workers' compensation insurance and its detailed regulatory oversight to ensure market stability and consumer protection.

Worker's Compensation Insurance

One of the hallmarks of Pennsylvania's insurance landscape is its detailed regulations surrounding workers' compensation. The state requires all employers to provide this insurance, which covers medical costs and lost wages for employees injured on the job. Pennsylvania's approach ensures quick and fair compensation for workers, reducing the need for litigation and helping employees return to work more swiftly.

Furthermore, Pennsylvania offers incentives for businesses that implement workplace safety measures, such as discounts on insurance premiums, underscoring the state's commitment to preventing workplace injuries before they occur.

Comprehensive Regulatory Framework

The Pennsylvania Insurance Department rigorously oversees all insurance activities within the state, ensuring that companies are financially healthy and operate in line with fair practices. This oversight includes periodic reviews of insurance products and rates, and stringent requirements for company solvency.

Consumer protections are also a significant focus, with the state mandating clear disclosure of insurance terms and prompt claims handling. These regulations are designed to prevent abuses in the insurance market and to provide recourse for consumers who feel their rights have been violated.

Pennsylvania insurance professionals must be well-versed in the state's regulatory requirements, particularly concerning workers' compensation and consumer protections. The state's proactive regulatory approach ensures that insurance practices are fair and transparent and that the insurance market remains stable and reliable.

Ohio's Insurance Regulatory Environment: Focused on Transparency and Consumer Protection

Ohio's insurance industry is strongly characterized by an emphasis on transparency and consumer education, ensuring that policyholders are well-informed and protected. This focus helps foster a reliable, consumer-friendly market where residents can confidently make insurance decisions.

Transparent Insurance Practices

Ohio mandates clear communication of insurance terms and conditions. Insurers must provide consumers with detailed policy information, ensuring they understand coverage limits, exclusions, and their rights under the policy. This transparency is critical in helping consumers decide about their insurance needs.

Consumer Education and Resources

The Ohio Department of Insurance (ODI) offers extensive resources to educate consumers about different types of insurance, including health, auto, life, and homeowners insurance. These resources are designed to empower consumers, helping them to understand how insurance works, what to look for in a policy, and how to file a claim.

Regular Market Conduct Examinations

Ohio conducts rigorous market conduct examinations to ensure that insurance companies comply with state laws and regulations. These examinations assess practices related to policy issuance, rate setting, complaint handling, and claims processing. Ensuring compliance helps maintain the integrity of the insurance market and protects consumer interests.

Advocacy for Consumer Rights

Ohio's regulatory framework includes strong advocacy for consumer rights. The ODI operates a consumer complaints division that assists policyholders in resolving disputes with insurers. This service is invaluable in holding insurers accountable and ensuring that consumer grievances are addressed fairly and promptly.

Impact of Transparency on Insurance Operations

The emphasis on transparency protects consumers and benefits the insurance market by promoting trust and stability. Insurers in Ohio are encouraged to compete based on service quality and value rather than through obscure pricing or complex terms.

For insurance professionals working in Ohio, a thorough understanding of the state's focus on transparency and consumer protection is crucial. These professionals must be adept at explaining intricate insurance details to clients and ensuring their practices align with state regulations. Ohio's regulatory environment supports a market where consumer rights are paramount and insurance education is a priority.

Michigan's insurance landscape, particularly its auto insurance sector, has undergone significant reforms to decrease costs and increase the flexibility and affordability of coverage for residents. The changes are substantial, with implications for every state's insurance system stakeholder.

Overview of Recent Reforms

Michigan's recent overhaul of its auto insurance system was driven by the need to address the state's historically high insurance rates. Reforms introduced choices in personal injury protection (PIP) coverage and established a fee schedule for medical providers. These changes aim to reduce the costs associated with auto insurance claims and premiums.

Choice in Personal Injury Protection

One of the most significant changes allows Michigan drivers to choose their level of PIP coverage. Previously, Michigan required unlimited PIP coverage, leading to high premiums. Now, consumers can select from levels of coverage that best suit their personal needs and financial situations, potentially lowering their costs.

Fee Schedules and Fraud Prevention

Introducing a fee schedule for medical services related to auto accidents helps control previously unchecked costs. Additionally, the state has enhanced measures to combat insurance fraud, further aiming to reduce unnecessary expenditures in the system.

Impact on Consumers and Insurers

These reforms are expected to provide more affordable options for consumers. At the same time, insurers adjust to a market where premium prices will likely be more competitive. The changes require insurers to reevaluate their pricing strategies and coverage offerings to remain competitive in the newly structured market.

Ongoing Adjustments and Market Adaptation

As the market adapts to these reforms, continuous monitoring and adjustments are likely necessary to ensure the objectives of reduced costs and increased coverage flexibility are met. The Michigan Department of Insurance and Financial Services plays a critical role in overseeing this transition and ensuring that the reforms benefit consumers without compromising insurers' financial stability.

For insurance professionals in Michigan, staying informed about the details and implications of the recent auto insurance reforms is essential. They must be prepared to guide their clients through the new options and help them make informed decisions about their auto insurance coverage. The evolving landscape offers both challenges and opportunities to enhance service offerings and consumer satisfaction in Michigan's insurance market.

North Carolina's approach to insurance regulation is heavily influenced by its geographic and climatic conditions, particularly the risks posed by hurricanes and floods. The state's insurance policies and regulations are designed to manage these risks effectively while ensuring that the insurance market remains robust and accessible.

Geographical Challenges and Insurance Implications

Located on the Atlantic coast, North Carolina is frequently in the path of hurricanes and tropical storms, which can cause significant property damage. The state's insurance regulations are tailored to address these challenges, focusing on maintaining affordability and ensuring sufficient coverage is available to those in high-risk areas.

Rate Setting and Regulatory Oversight

The North Carolina Department of Insurance is active in the rate-setting process, particularly for homeowners and auto insurance. This involvement is critical to prevent rising premiums in coastal areas with higher risks. The state employs a unique methodology for assessing insurance rates, incorporating actuarial data and regional risk factors considerations.

Flood Insurance and Natural Disaster Preparedness

In addition to standard insurance policies, North Carolina promotes the purchase of flood insurance and has implemented measures to improve natural disaster preparedness and response. The state works closely with insurers to ensure that they are adequately prepared to handle claims and support recovery efforts following major storms.

Consumer Protection and Market Stability

North Carolina strongly emphasizes consumer protection, with regulations designed to ensure fair treatment of policyholders and prevent abuses in the market. The state also supports efforts to educate consumers about their insurance options and the importance of adequate coverage, particularly concerning the natural risks involved.

Insurance professionals in North Carolina must be well-versed in the state's specific regulatory environment, particularly regarding natural disasters and rate setting. Understanding these local nuances enables professionals to serve their clients better and contribute to a stable, fair, and resilient insurance market. The strategic management of insurance regulations in North Carolina showcases a commitment to both consumer protection and industry sustainability, making it a model for other states with similar geographic and climatic challenges.

Claims Handling Process: From First Notice of Loss to Resolution

The claims handling process is critical to insurance operations, directly impacting customer satisfaction and trust. It begins with the first notice of loss (FNOL). It ends with the resolution of the claim, encompassing several critical steps designed to evaluate, process, and settle claims efficiently and fairly.

1. **First Notice of Loss**: This is the initial report made by the policyholder following a loss. Timely and accurate FNOL is crucial as it sets the stage for the entire claims process. Insurers often provide multiple channels, such as online forms, mobile apps, and 24/7 call centers, to facilitate prompt reporting.

2. **Claim Assessment**: Once the FNOL is received, insurers assign a claims adjuster to assess the claim. This involves reviewing the policy to confirm coverage, investigating the circumstances of the loss, evaluating damages, and determining the insurer's liability.

3. **Adjustment Process**: The adjuster may need to visit the loss site, gather witnesses' statements, and collect further documentation from the policyholder. Modern tools like drone technology and virtual assessments can expedite this process and enhance accuracy.

4. **Resolution and Payout**: After assessing the claim, the adjuster proposes a settlement based on the policy terms and the evaluated damages. If the policyholder accepts the settlement offer, the insurer processes the payment, thereby resolving the claim.

5. **Follow-up**: Post-claim resolution, insurers often follow up with the claimant to ensure satisfaction and address any additional concerns, helping to maintain a positive relationship and trust between the insurer and the policyholder.

Adjusting Claims: Techniques and Ethical Considerations

Adjusting claims involves technical know-how and ethical considerations to ensure fair treatment of all parties involved. Claims adjusters are on the front lines, interpreting the policy and assessing claims against it.

1. **Accuracy and Objectivity**: Adjusters must evaluate claims based on the facts presented and the coverage stipulated in the policy without personal bias influencing their decisions.

2. **Communication**: Clear and ongoing communication with the claimant is vital. Adjusters should keep the policyholder informed about the status of their claim and any requirements or issues that arise.

3. **Confidentiality**: Respecting the privacy of claimants and safeguarding their personal information is crucial.

4. **Anti-Fraud Measures**: Adjusters must be vigilant against fraudulent claims, which involves recognizing signs of fraud and conducting thorough investigations.

5. **Ethical Negotiations**: In negotiating settlements, adjusters must adhere to ethical standards, ensuring that offers are fair and comply with the insurance policy's terms.

Subrogation in Insurance: Process and Implications

Subrogation is a process where an insurer seeks recovery of the amount paid to the insured from a third party that caused the loss. This process helps lower insurance premiums by recovering costs that the insurer should not bear.

1. **Initiation of Subrogation**: After compensating the insured, an insurer steps into their shoes to claim damages from the responsible party or their insurer.

2. **Legal Rights**: The insurer may need to pursue legal action to recover the damages. This requires careful documentation and sometimes negotiation with the third party or their insurer.

3. **Impact on Insured**: Policyholders should be aware that participating in the subrogation process can affect their claim and potential recovery.

Insurance Fraud: Detection and Prevention Strategies

Insurance fraud poses significant costs to the industry and policyholders. Effective detection and prevention strategies are critical.

1. **Data Analytics**: Advanced analytics can identify patterns indicative of fraud, helping insurers preemptively address suspicious activities.

2. **Training**: Educating employees and agents to recognize fraud can lead to early detection and preventive measures.

3. **Collaboration**: Insurers often work with law enforcement and other insurers to combat fraud, sharing intelligence and best practices.

Appraisal vs. Arbitration: Roles in Claim Resolution

Claim disputes may be resolved through appraisal or arbitration, depending on the policy terms.

1. **Appraisal**: Used to resolve disputes about the value of a claim, where each party chooses an appraiser and a third party makes a binding decision.

2. **Arbitration**: Involves a neutral arbitrator who makes a binding decision on the broader aspects of a claim dispute, not just the value.

Both mechanisms provide alternatives to litigation, offering a faster resolution to disputes within the bounds of the insurance policy.

Catastrophe Management: Insuring Against Disasters

Catastrophe management in insurance involves planning and response strategies that minimize disasters' financial impact on insurers and policyholders. Effective management is crucial in regions prone to natural disasters such as hurricanes, floods, and earthquakes.

1. **Risk Assessment and Modeling**: Insurers use sophisticated models to predict the likelihood and potential impact of disasters on their insured assets. This helps set premiums that accurately reflect the risk and determine the necessary reserves to cover potential claims.

2. **Disaster Response Plans**: Insurers develop comprehensive disaster response plans that outline how they will support policyholders in the aftermath of a catastrophe. These plans include mobilizing claims adjusters to the affected areas quickly and setting up temporary claims offices if necessary.

3. **Partnerships with Emergency Services**: Collaboration with local and national emergency services ensures a coordinated response during disasters. Insurers often work closely with these agencies to provide immediate assistance to policyholders.

4. **Education and Preparedness Programs**: Insurers invest in community education programs that teach policyholders how to protect their properties and what steps to take immediately following a disaster. These programs are crucial for mitigating losses and expediting the recovery process.

5. **Reinsurance to Manage Risk**: Reinsurance agreements allow insurers to transfer a portion of their risk, ensuring they are not overly exposed to a single catastrophic event. This financial tool is essential for maintaining insurer solvency and stability in the face of large-scale disasters.

The Concept of Vacant vs. Unoccupied in Insurance Policies

Understanding the distinction between vacant and unoccupied properties is essential for both insurers and policyholders, as it affects coverage decisions and risk assessment.

1. **Vacant Properties**: A property is considered vacant when it is empty and devoid of personal property. Insurance policies typically restrict coverage for vacant properties due to the higher risk of vandalism, theft, and unnoticed damages that can escalate, such as water leaks.

2. **Unoccupied Properties**: A property is unoccupied if it has furnishings and the owner intends to return. Unoccupied homes may face similar risks as vacant ones but to a lesser extent. Insurers may allow a grace period for unoccupied properties before certain coverages are restricted.

3. **Special Endorsements**: Property owners can purchase endorsements to cover vacancies or extended periods of unoccupancy. These endorsements are crucial for maintaining coverage during renovations, extended trips away from home, or the transition between tenants in a rental property.

4. **Risk Mitigation**: Insurers advise policyholders on ways to mitigate risks associated with vacant or unoccupied properties, such as regular property checks, installing security systems, and managing utilities to prevent damage.

Burglary, Robbery, and Theft: Insurance Definitions and Claims

Burglary, robbery, and theft are distinct terms with specific meanings in the context of insurance, and understanding these definitions helps in the accurate processing of claims.

1. **Burglary**: Defined as breaking and entering into a structure unlawfully, intending to commit a felony, usually theft. Insurance policies require evidence of forced entry for a claim to be classified under burglary.

2. **Robbery**: Involves taking property from a person with intent to permanently deprive them of it through force or fear. Robbery claims are processed under personal property coverage if the policyholder is threatened or harmed during the incident.

3. **Theft** is a broader term that includes stealing property without the owner's consent. Theft can occur without the elements of force or unlawful entry, such as in cases of pickpocketing or shoplifting.

4. **Claim Processing**: Insurers require detailed incident documentation, including police reports, evidence of forced entry, and lists of stolen items. These details are crucial for verifying the claim and determining the settlement amount.

PART VI: MARKET DYNAMICS AND ADVANCED CONSIDERATIONS

The Insurance Market: Understanding Its Structure and Dynamics

The insurance market, encompassing a wide range of coverage from property and casualty to life and health, operates within a complex framework shaped by economic, regulatory, and technological forces. Understanding its structure and dynamics is essential for navigating effectively within the industry.

Market Structure: The insurance industry is segmented into various sectors, including direct insurers, reinsurers, brokers, and now insurtech companies. Direct insurers handle the underwriting and sale of policies to individuals or companies. Reinsurers provide risk management for insurers, taking on a portion of the risk in exchange for part of the premiums. Brokers and agents facilitate the sale of policies by advising clients on the best coverage options to suit their needs.

Regulatory Environment: Each state in the U.S. has its own insurance department that regulates operations within its borders, leading to a patchwork of laws and regulations. This decentralized regulatory system requires insurers to navigate differing compliance challenges across states. Furthermore, international markets are governed by additional bodies such as the International Association of Insurance Supervisors (IAIS), adding another layer of complexity.

Economic Impact: The economic environment significantly influences the insurance market. Factors such as interest rates, inflation, and economic growth affect insurers' investment returns and the overall demand for insurance products. For instance, higher interest rates can improve the yield on the investment portfolios of insurers, enhancing their capacity to underwrite new policies. Conversely, an economic downturn might reduce demand for certain types of insurance as consumers and businesses tighten budgets.

Consumer Behavior: Technological advancements and shifting consumer expectations drive changes in how insurance products are developed and marketed. Customers now demand more transparency, customized products, and seamless service delivery facilitated by digital platforms. Insurers are responding by leveraging big data analytics to gain insights into consumer behavior and preferences, which allows for more targeted and efficient product offerings.

Globalization: The insurance market is increasingly global in scope. Multinational insurers face opportunities and challenges in entering new markets, each with its regulatory landscape and market conditions. Globalization also exposes insurers to cross-border risks, such as international regulatory changes or economic crises, requiring sophisticated risk management strategies.

The interplay of diverse elements including regulation, economics, consumer behavior, and technology heightens the insurance market's complexity. Success in this industry depends on understanding these dynamics and adapting strategies accordingly. Insurers must stay informed and agile, ready to evolve with changing market conditions to meet the needs of their clients effectively.

National Association of Insurance Commissioners (NAIC): Role and Influence

The National Association of Insurance Commissioners (NAIC) plays a pivotal role in the U.S. insurance industry, acting as a standard-setting and regulatory support organization created and governed by the chief insurance regulators from the 50 states, the District of Columbia, and five U.S. territories. Its mission is to provide state insurance regulators with the tools and resources to regulate the industry effectively and protect consumers.

Standardization and Uniformity: One of the primary functions of the NAIC is to promote uniformity across state insurance regulations. This is achieved through the development of model laws and regulations, which states can choose to adopt. The model regulations cover various insurance activities, from company licensing to rate filings and policyholder protections. By promoting uniformity, the NAIC helps ensure that insurance companies can operate across state lines more seamlessly, reducing administrative burdens and fostering a more competitive market environment.

Consumer Protection: The NAIC is heavily focused on protecting the interests of insurance consumers. It develops standards and regulatory frameworks to ensure fair treatment of policyholders. It provides resources to educate consumers about their rights and the basics of insurance. The NAIC's Consumer Information Source (CIS) offers tools for policyholders to check insurance companies' financial health and understand the coverage options available to them.

Regulatory Support and Innovation: The NAIC allows regulators to collaborate on best practices and emerging issues. This includes the development of solutions for new risks such as cybersecurity threats and the implications of technological advancements like autonomous vehicles and artificial intelligence in insurance. The NAIC also facilitates training and education for state insurance regulators, ensuring that they are well-equipped to manage new challenges in the industry.

Data Collection and Analysis: The organization collects and analyzes a vast amount of insurance data, which is used to monitor the health of the insurance industry, assist in regulatory activities, and provide transparency. This data is critical for assessing market trends and insurer solvency and supporting actuarial studies.

International Influence: While primarily focused on the U.S., the NAIC also interacts with international regulatory bodies to align global insurance regulations and to manage the complexities of multinational insurers and reinsurers. This global engagement helps ensure that U.S. insurance regulations are harmonious with international standards, which is crucial in a globally connected market.

Conclusion: The NAIC's role in shaping and supporting the U.S. insurance regulatory landscape is fundamental. Through its efforts to ensure uniformity, protect consumers, support innovation, and collaborate internationally, the NAIC helps maintain a stable, competitive, and fair insurance market that can adapt to changing global and domestic challenges.

The Use of Technology in Insurance: Trends and Future Directions

The insurance sector is increasingly influenced by technology, which has transformed traditional practices and introduced new efficiencies and capabilities. This shift is driven by technological advancements that reshape how insurers engage with customers, process claims, and assess risks. The impact of technology in insurance, often referred to as "Insurtech," is profound and expanding, promising a future where insurance is more personalized, efficient, and integrated into daily life.

Big Data and Advanced Analytics: One of the most significant technological advancements in insurance is using big data and analytics. Insurers collect vast amounts of data from various sources, including telematics, IoT devices, social media, and more. This data is analyzed to gain detailed insights into customer behavior, preferences, and risk profiles. For instance, auto insurers use telematics data to monitor driving behaviors, such as speed, braking habits, and time of day on the road, to offer personalized premium rates based on actual driving performance. Similarly, property insurers utilize data from smart home devices to monitor for risks like leaks or unauthorized entries, potentially preventing incidents before they occur.

Artificial Intelligence and Machine Learning: AI and machine learning revolutionize claim processing and customer service. AI algorithms can automate routine claims handling, reducing processing times from days to minutes and increasing accuracy by minimizing human error. Furthermore, powered by AI, chatbots and virtual assistants provide 24/7 customer service, handling inquiries and claims notifications efficiently, enhancing customer satisfaction and engagement.

Blockchain Technology: Blockchain offers transformative potential for the insurance industry by enabling more secure, transparent, and efficient transactions. Smart contracts, self-executing contractual states stored on the blockchain, automate claims and payments, reducing the possibility of fraud and decreasing administrative costs. For example, in travel insurance, smart contracts can automatically trigger compensation to customers whose flights are delayed without requiring manual claim submissions.

Cybersecurity: As insurers adopt more digital technologies, the importance of cybersecurity escalates. Protecting sensitive customer data against breaches and cyber-attacks is paramount. Insurers are investing in advanced security technologies, including encryption and blockchain, and adopting stricter data governance practices to safeguard information integrity and compliance with regulations like GDPR.

Looking ahead, the integration of technology in insurance is set to deepen. The Internet of Things (IoT) will play a larger role in monitoring and preventing risks in real-time. For instance, wearable devices could help life insurers track policyholders' health metrics, offering incentives for maintaining a healthy lifestyle. Similarly, adopting 5G technology will enhance the capabilities of IoT devices and mobile solutions, further transforming customer interactions and data collection.

The ongoing evolution of technology in insurance not only enhances operational efficiencies but also provides a more tailored and proactive approach to customer needs. As technology advances, insurers who embrace these innovations will lead the market, offering superior products and services that meet the expectations of a digitally connected consumer base.

Cyber Insurance: Emerging Risks and Coverages

Cyber insurance has become a critical component of risk management strategies as businesses and individuals increasingly rely on digital technologies and face growing cyber threats. This insurance type addresses losses related to data breaches, hacking incidents, and other cyber-related security issues.

Emerging Risks: The cyber landscape continuously evolves, presenting new risks such as ransomware attacks, where attackers encrypt an organization's data and demand payment for its release. Phishing attacks and social engineering scams are also on the rise, tricking employees into revealing confidential information. Additionally, the increasing connectivity of devices introduces vulnerabilities in areas previously considered low-risk, expanding the potential for cyber-attacks across a broader array of industries.

Coverage Specifics: Cyber insurance policies typically cover a range of expenses associated with cyber incidents, including the costs of notifying affected individuals, legal fees, fines, and penalties, as well as the expenses related to recovering compromised data and repairing damaged systems. Cyber insurance also covers business interruption losses, compensating for income lost due to a cyber event.

Challenges in Coverage: One of the significant challenges in cyber insurance is the difficulty in quantifying risk due to the lack of historical data and the rapid evolution of cyber threats. This makes pricing policies and determining coverage limits challenging. Insurers must continuously adapt their policies to reflect the current threat landscape and ensure they are providing adequate protection.

Regulatory Considerations: As cyber threats become more prominent, regulatory bodies worldwide are implementing stricter data protection laws, such as the EU's General Data Protection Regulation (GDPR) and the California Consumer Privacy Act (CCPA) in the U.S. These regulations increase the liability for companies handling personal data, driving the need for comprehensive cyber insurance coverage.

As dependency on digital technologies grows, the demand for cyber insurance is expected to rise. Insurers are responding by developing more sophisticated risk assessment models and tailoring their products to meet the specific needs of different industries and businesses. Moreover, there is a growing trend towards integrating cybersecurity services with cyber insurance policies, providing clients with preventative measures alongside financial protection.

Cyber insurance is a dynamic and essential field within the insurance industry, requiring insurers to stay abreast of technological advancements and regulatory changes. As cyber risks continue to evolve, the insurance industry must innovate and expand its offerings to provide effective protection against these pervasive threats, ensuring stability and security in an increasingly digital world.

Marine and Inland Marine Insurance: Scope and Coverage

Marine and inland marine insurance are crucial insurance industry segments, providing essential coverage for transporting goods over water and land and insuring specialized properties. These insurance types are vital for shipping, logistics, and even construction businesses, where goods, equipment, or materials must be protected against transit and storage risks.

Marine Insurance

Marine insurance traditionally covers the loss or damage of ships, cargo, terminals, and any property by which cargo is transferred, acquired, or held between the points of origin and final destination. This type of insurance is divided into two main categories: hull and machinery (H&M) and cargo insurance. H&M insurance covers the vessel itself from damages incurred during maritime operations, while cargo insurance covers the goods transported on the vessel. Key risks include perils of the sea (such as storms and collisions), piracy, and other navigational hazards. Policies are typically tailored to the specific needs of the shipowner or cargo owner, with premiums adjusted based on the route, nature of goods, and history of losses.

Inland Marine Insurance: Despite its name, inland marine insurance has nothing to do with marine activities. It originally insured goods transported over inland waterways but has evolved to cover goods in transit on land and certain types of movable property. This includes goods transported by truck or train, construction equipment, mobile equipment, and properties that involve an element of transportation. Inland marine insurance is particularly important for industries that rely on the transport of expensive or large quantities of goods. Coverage can extend to include theft, fire, wind, collision, and other perils, depending on the policy.

Unique Coverage Needs: Both types of insurance address needs not typically met by standard commercial property policies. For example, a construction company might use inland marine insurance to cover a crane or other equipment that is being moved from one job site to another. Similarly, a museum might use it to insure pieces of art being transported to an exhibition.

Underwriting Challenges: Underwriting these types of insurance requires specialized knowledge of the industries involved. Underwriters must consider various factors, including the nature of the goods or equipment insured, the conditions under which they will be transported, and the potential hazards they might encounter. The values at risk, the historical loss experience of the transport operator, and even international political conditions can affect policy terms and pricing.

Regulatory Aspects: Like other insurance types, marine and inland marine insurance are subject to regulatory oversight, but they also involve international laws and conventions, especially in cross-border transactions. Insurers must navigate these complex legal landscapes to ensure compliance and adequate risk management.

Marine and inland marine insurance play a critical role in global commerce and other sectors by mitigating the risks associated with transportation and movable properties. As global trade continues to expand and as assets become increasingly mobile, the relevance of these insurance types grows, driving the need for sophisticated risk assessment and innovative insurance solutions.

Aviation Insurance: Key Concepts and Coverage

Aviation insurance covers risks associated with aircraft operations and other aviation-related activities. This type of insurance is vital for airlines, aircraft owners, manufacturers, and service providers in the aviation sector. Given the high-risk nature of aviation, the stakes involved in ensuring such operations are immense, involving complex liability issues, high-value assets, and unique risks.

Coverage Types: Aviation insurance can be broadly categorized into several types, including hull insurance, liability insurance, and personal accident insurance. Hull insurance covers physical damage to the aircraft itself, whether on the ground or in the air. Liability insurance covers the aircraft operator's legal liabilities towards third parties, resulting from acts such as property damage or bodily injuries caused by an aircraft or its operations. Personal accident insurance covers the crew and passengers, offering benefits in the event of injuries or death.

Underwriting Considerations: Underwriting aviation insurance requires a deep understanding of aviation technology, operations, and the specific use of the aircraft. Insurers consider factors such as the type and age of the aircraft, the qualifications and experience of the pilots, and the maintenance schedule of the aircraft. Furthermore, the geographical areas over which the aircraft operates can significantly affect risk levels, especially in regions prone to conflict or natural disasters.

Claims and Risks: Aviation insurance claims can be highly complex and involve substantial financial amounts. Insurers must adeptly handle claims related to aircraft accidents, which may involve multiple jurisdictions and detailed investigations. The risk of catastrophic losses is significant in aviation insurance, prompting insurers to employ rigorous risk management and claims handling procedures.

Market Dynamics: The aviation insurance market is cyclical, with periods of high profitability followed by phases where losses may exceed premiums. This cycle is influenced by factors such as global economic conditions, technological advancements in aviation, and changes in regulatory frameworks.

Emerging Trends: Recent trends affecting aviation insurance include the increasing use of drones and unmanned aerial vehicles (UAVs), which introduce new types of exposures and demand novel insurance solutions. The evolving nature of threats, such as cyber-attacks targeting aircraft systems and data, also compels the aviation insurance sector to innovate continually.

Aviation insurance is a dynamic field that requires insurers to constantly update their knowledge and strategies to keep pace with technological advancements and changing market conditions. Adequate coverage in this sector protects financial investments. It ensures the ongoing safety and security of global aviation operations, underscoring the critical role of insurance in this high-stakes industry.

Directors and Officers (D&O) Liability Insurance

Directors and Officers (D&O) Liability Insurance is a specialized form of coverage designed to protect the personal assets of corporate directors and officers and the financial health of their organizations from claims resulting from alleged or actual wrongful acts they may have committed in their positions. As the regulatory landscape becomes more stringent and litigious activities more prevalent, the importance of D&O insurance in corporate risk management strategies has grown significantly.

Scope and Importance of D&O Insurance

Coverage Basics: D&O insurance policies offer financial protection to directors and officers of corporations against legal judgments and costs arising from various wrongful acts, including breaches of duty, neglect, error, misstatements, or misleading statements. Without such coverage, the personal assets of corporate leaders could be at risk, which could also hinder the ability to attract qualified individuals to these critical roles.

Key Risks Covered: This type of insurance primarily covers management liability, but it can also extend to protect the company in cases where it indemnifies its managers for costs incurred during legal proceedings. Additionally, D&O policies can cover the corporate entity itself when it is named in a lawsuit against its directors and officers.

Claims Examples: Common claims under D&O policies include breach of fiduciary duty, failure to comply with regulations (leading to regulatory fines and penalties), misrepresentation of company assets, misuse of company funds, fraud, and the failure to disclose material information to shareholders.

Evolution and Market Dynamics

The D&O insurance market has evolved significantly over the years, influenced by changes in corporate governance, increasing shareholder activism, and a heightened awareness of environmental, social, and governance (ESG) issues. As a result, insurers have adapted their offerings to cover more complex scenarios and emerging risks, including cyber liabilities and reputational damage.

Globalization Impact: As businesses expand operations internationally, directors and officers face an increasingly complex array of international laws and regulations. This global reach necessitates D&O policies that provide worldwide coverage and are capable of addressing diverse legal environments and potential claims from various jurisdictions.

Pricing and Capacity: D&O insurance is susceptible to market conditions. In times of economic downturn or increased litigation, premiums can rise, and policy terms may tighten. Conversely, coverage can become more affordable in a soft market, and terms may be more favorable to policyholders. Insurers continually assess their exposure to align pricing with perceived risk levels, which can fluctuate based on economic, legal, and social trends.

Challenges and Considerations

Underwriting Complexity: Underwriting D&O insurance is complex and requires a deep understanding of the company's financial health, management practices, industry-specific risks, and the regulatory environment. Underwriters must assess the potential for claims based on various factors, including the company's operational history, its sector, the experience and track records of its executives, and the effectiveness of its corporate governance structures.

Claims Severity and Frequency: While D&O claims may be less frequent than other types of insurance claims, they can be severe in terms of potential financial damage. High-profile cases involving fiduciary duties or corporate mismanagement breaches can lead to multimillion-dollar settlements, making the stakes for D&O insurers particularly high.

Regulatory Changes: Ongoing changes in corporate law and securities regulations can alter the risk landscape rapidly. Directors and officers must stay informed about these changes to mitigate risks proactively. Insurers, too, must keep abreast of legal trends to adjust their policies accordingly and ensure adequate coverage.

The Role of D&O Insurance in Modern Corporate Strategy

In today's business environment, where the actions of a company's leadership are under intense scrutiny, D&O insurance plays a critical role in corporate strategy. It provides a safety net against potential claims and acts as a mechanism to attract and retain top talent. Executives and board members are more likely to take on the risks associated with leadership roles when they know they are protected against personal liability.

Risk Management Tool

Beyond financial protection, D&O insurance is essential to a company's overall risk management strategy. It encourages better governance and risk management practices by incentivizing compliance and ethical corporate conduct. Insurers often provide guidance and training as part of their D&O offerings, helping firms improve their governance practices and reduce the likelihood of claims.

The future of D&O insurance will likely be shaped by increasing digitalization, the rise of artificial intelligence, and changes in the legal environment concerning director and officer responsibilities. Insurers must continuously innovate to address these new risks and provide relevant, robust protection for today's corporate leaders.

Directors and Officers Liability Insurance is more than just a financial safeguard; it's a critical component of modern corporate governance and risk management frameworks. As the business and regulatory landscapes continue to evolve, D&O insurance will remain a dynamic and indispensable tool for companies looking to navigate the complexities of corporate leadership and responsibility effectively.

Workers' Compensation: Coverage and Claims Process

Workers' compensation is a critical component of the insurance landscape, providing financial and medical benefits to employees who suffer job-related injuries or illnesses. This insurance type is mandatory in most jurisdictions, ensuring workers are protected against the financial hardships associated with workplace accidents and protecting employers from costly lawsuits.

Legal Framework and Coverage: Workers' compensation laws are enacted at the state level, which means the specifics can vary significantly from one state to another. However, the general principle remains that employers must provide coverage that includes medical expenses, rehabilitation costs, and a portion of the employee's wages during the period they cannot work. In exchange, employees relinquish the right to sue their employer for negligence, creating a no-fault framework to benefit both parties.

Claims Process: The claims process begins when an employee reports an injury or illness to their employer, usually within a specified time frame after the incident. The employer then must file a claim with their workers' compensation insurance carrier. The insurer assesses the claim to determine the insurance coverage's validity and extent. Approved claims result in benefits being paid to the injured or ill employee to cover medical costs and lost wages.

Complexity in Claims: Determining the extent of an injury and its connection to the workplace can be complex. Disputes may arise over the nature of the injury, the appropriate treatment, and the amount of benefits due. In such cases, the claims process can involve negotiations between the insurer, the employer, and the employee and may even require legal intervention to resolve.

Preventative Measures: Many workers' compensation insurers work closely with employers to develop workplace safety programs that reduce the risk of injuries. These programs can be highly effective in lowering the number of claims and can also help reduce insurance premiums by minimizing risk.

Role of Workers' Compensation in Employee Safety: Beyond providing financial benefits, workers' compensation promotes safe work practices and environments. By requiring employers to invest in safety and by fostering a quicker return to work, workers' compensation insurance supports both economic and health outcomes for employees.

Professional Liability Insurance: Errors and Omissions

Professional liability insurance, also known as Errors and Omissions (E&O) insurance, is designed to protect professionals and businesses against liability incurred as a result of errors and omissions in providing professional services. This type of insurance is particularly crucial for professionals who provide advice or services, such as lawyers, accountants, architects, and engineers.

Coverage Specifics: E&O insurance helps cover the legal costs and settlements that may arise from claims of professional negligence, missed deadlines, undelivered services, or mistakes in the service provided. Unlike general liability insurance, which covers bodily injury or property damage, E&O insurance addresses financial loss and other damages directly related to the professional service provided.

Importance of E&O Insurance: In today's litigious environment, the risk of being sued for negligence is significant, even if no mistake has been made. E&O insurance provides peace of mind for professionals, ensuring they can defend themselves against claims without jeopardizing their financial stability.

Claims-Made Coverage: Most E&O policies are "claims-made," meaning they only cover claims made during the policy period. Professionals must maintain continuous coverage to ensure protection, and any gaps in coverage can be risky.

Risk Management: Insurers often provide risk management services to help insured professionals minimize the likelihood of a claim. This can include training in best practices, contract review services, and proactive communication strategies to help prevent client disputes before they escalate into claims.

The Evolving Nature of E&O Insurance: As professions evolve and new types of services emerge, E&O insurance must adapt to cover new risks. For example, with the rise of technology and internet services, there is a growing need for E&O insurance that addresses cyber liability and data protection issues.

Workers' compensation and professional liability insurance are essential elements of the broader insurance landscape, each addressing specific needs related to workplace safety and professional services. These insurance types protect against financial losses and support workers' and professionals' health, safety, and stability in various industries. As market dynamics shift and new risks emerge, these insurance sectors will continue to evolve, playing a crucial role in risk management and economic security.

SECTION II
MULTIPLE CHOICE QUESTIONS

GENERAL QUESTIONS

Question 1: What does a "Claims-made" policy in Professional Liability Insurance cover?

A) Claims filed during the policy period, regardless of when the event occurred.
B) Claims arising from incidents that occur during the policy period, regardless of when the claim is filed.
C) Claims reported and incidents that occur only after the policy has been purchased.
D) All claims related to professional services provided within the policy period.

Correct Answer: A) Claims filed during the policy period, regardless of when the event occurred.

Explanation: A "Claims-made" policy provides coverage for claims that are actually filed during the policy period, regardless of when the wrongful act that gave rise to the claim occurred. This is distinct from an "Occurrence" policy, which covers incidents that occur during the policy period, no matter when the claim is eventually made. Understanding this distinction is crucial for professionals who need to manage their liability risks effectively, ensuring they maintain continuous coverage to protect against claims from past professional activities.

Question 2: What is the primary purpose of Directors and Officers (D&O) Liability Insurance?

A) To cover physical damages to the property of a business.
B) To protect directors and officers from personal losses due to workplace injuries.
C) To protect directors and officers from personal liabilities arising from their corporate actions.
D) To provide health insurance benefits to directors and officers.

Correct Answer: C) To protect directors and officers from personal liabilities arising from their corporate actions.

Explanation: Directors and Officers Liability Insurance is designed to shield corporate directors and officers from personal financial losses if they are sued as a result of performing their duties as they relate to the company. This insurance covers legal fees, settlements, and other costs associated with defending against lawsuits that claim wrongful acts in their capacity as directors or officers. This coverage is crucial for attracting and maintaining qualified individuals in these high-stakes roles.

Question 3: How does the concept of 'Subrogation' function in property and casualty insurance?

A) It allows an insurer to take legal action in the name of the insured to recover damages paid out.
B) It provides insurers the right to increase premiums after a claim is paid.
C) It permits the insured to claim twice for the same loss from different policies.
D) It involves the insured reimbursing the insurer for claims expenses.

Correct Answer: A) It allows an insurer to take legal action in the name of the insured to recover damages paid out.

Explanation: Subrogation in insurance refers to the process by which an insurer can pursue a third party that caused an insurance loss to the insured. This is done in an attempt to recover the amount of the claim paid to the insured for the loss. Subrogation is a key element in insurance policies that helps mitigate claims costs and keep insurance premiums more affordable for all policyholders.

Question 4: What does 'Coinsurance' in a property insurance policy entail?

A) A split in risk between two insurance companies.
B) A requirement that the insured must bear a portion of the loss.
C) A mandatory co-payment by the insured on all claims processed.
D) The insured and insurer share the policy premium costs equally.

Correct Answer: B) A requirement that the insured must bear a portion of the loss.

Explanation: Coinsurance in property insurance is a clause used to encourage policyholders to insure their property to a value close to its actual replacement cost. Under a coinsurance clause, if the insured has purchased less coverage than required, they must bear a portion of any loss proportionally. This is calculated based on the percentage of coverage purchased compared to what was required.

Question 5: Which policy feature specifically addresses the risks associated with vacant or unoccupied properties?

A) Liability endorsement
B) Vacancy permit
C) All-risk coverage
D) Business interruption insurance

Correct Answer: B) Vacancy permit

Explanation: A vacancy permit is an endorsement to a property insurance policy that provides coverage for properties that are vacant or unoccupied for extended periods. Since these properties are at higher risk for incidents such as vandalism or unnoticed damages, standard policies may not provide full coverage without such an endorsement.

Question 6: What role does the National Association of Insurance Commissioners (NAIC) play in the insurance industry?

A) It directly sells insurance to consumers.
B) It sets mandatory federal standards for all insurance policies.
C) It provides resources, expertise, and regulatory support to state insurance regulators.
D) It manages the liquidation of bankrupt insurance companies.

Correct Answer: C) It provides state insurance regulators with resources, expertise, and regulatory support.

Explanation: The National Association of Insurance Commissioners (NAIC) is an organization that helps state insurance regulators by developing model regulations, providing regulatory resources, and promoting uniformity. The NAIC does not sell insurance or handle bankruptcies directly but supports the state regulators overseeing these functions. This helps ensure a stable, effective, and consistent regulatory environment across the United States.

Question 7: What is the main difference between Named Peril and Open Peril insurance policies?

A) Named Peril policies cover all risks except those expressly excluded.
B) Open Peril policies cover only those risks named explicitly in the policy.
C) Named Peril policies cover only those risks named explicitly in the policy.
D) Open Peril policies do not provide coverage for natural disasters.

Correct Answer: C) Named Peril policies cover only those risks named explicitly in the policy.

Explanation: Named Peril policies offer coverage for only the risks that are explicitly listed within the policy document, such as fire, theft, or water damage. This is in contrast to Open Peril (or All Risks) policies, which cover all risks except for those that are specifically excluded. Understanding the distinction helps insureds know exactly what their policy protects against, enabling better risk management and coverage decisions.

Question 8: How does 'Actual Cash Value' differ from 'Replacement Cost' in property insurance?

A) Actual Cash Value includes depreciation, whereas Replacement Cost does not.
B) Replacement Cost includes depreciation, whereas Actual Cash Value does not.
C) Actual Cash Value covers temporary relocations, unlike Replacement Cost.
D) Replacement Cost only covers up to the item's original purchase price.

Correct Answer: A) Actual Cash Value includes depreciation, whereas Replacement Cost does not.

Explanation: Actual Cash Value (ACV) compensates the policyholder for the item's value at the time of the damage or loss, factoring in depreciation. Replacement Cost coverage, however, reimburses the full cost of replacing the lost or damaged item with a new one, without considering depreciation. This distinction is crucial for policyholders to understand to select the coverage type that best suits their needs.

Question 9: What is the primary purpose of Umbrella Insurance in personal liability coverage?

A) To provide initial coverage before basic policies activate.
B) To extend coverage limits beyond what is provided by standard policies.
C) To cover medical expenses that general health insurance does not.
D) To replace income in the event of temporary disability due to an accident.

Correct Answer: B) To extend coverage limits beyond what is provided by standard policies.

Explanation: Umbrella Insurance is a form of personal liability insurance that provides additional coverage beyond the limits of the policyholder's homeowners, auto, or watercraft insurance policies. It acts as a safety net by covering liabilities exceeding other policies' limits, protecting against major claims and lawsuits that could otherwise financially devastate an individual or family.

Question 10: In the context of Professional Liability Insurance, what does 'Tail Coverage' refer to?

A) Coverage that protects against claims made after a policy has expired.
B) An extension of coverage for newly hired professionals.
C) Insurance that covers the back end of a claim process, including appeals.
D) Additional coverage for the most common types of claims in a profession.

Correct Answer: A) Coverage that protects against claims made after a policy has expired.

Explanation: Tail Coverage, also known as Extended Reporting Period coverage, is an essential feature in claims-made insurance policies, particularly in professional liability insurance. It allows the insured to report claims to their insurer for a certain period after the policy has ended, provided the act occurred during the policy's effective period. This is particularly critical in professions where claims may be made long after the service is provided.

Question 11: What role does 'Deductible' play in an insurance policy?

A) It is the maximum amount an insurer will pay out in the event of a claim.
B) It is the amount the policyholder must pay out-of-pocket before the insurer pays a claim.
C) It is a mandatory fee paid annually for the policy renewal.
D) It determines the premium rate based on the policyholder's credit score.

Correct Answer: B) It is the amount the policyholder must pay out-of-pocket before the insurer pays a claim.

Explanation: A deductible is a cost-sharing mechanism in an insurance policy that dictates the amount a policyholder is responsible for paying out-of-pocket towards a claim before the insurance coverage kicks in. The purpose of a deductible is to mitigate minor claims and reduce the administrative costs for insurers while also encouraging policyholders to prevent small losses. Choosing a higher deductible can lower the policy's premium, as it increases the policyholder's share of the risk.

Question 12: What is the primary function of reinsurance in the insurance industry?

A) To increase the premium rates for high-risk policyholders.
B) To allow insurers to underwrite policies that exceed their risk capacities.
C) To directly sell insurance to consumers.
D) To act as a primary insurer for small-scale policies.

Correct Answer: B) To allow insurers to underwrite policies that exceed their risk capacities.

Explanation: Reinsurance is a mechanism primary insurers use to share the risks of large or potentially volatile policies with other insurance companies. This practice allows insurers to take on more significant policies while managing their risk exposure and capital requirements effectively. Reinsurance is critical in stabilizing the insurance market by spreading risk across multiple parties, ensuring that no single insurer faces overwhelming losses.

Question 13: How do state-specific insurance regulations influence underwriting practices?

A) They standardize underwriting practices across all states.
B) They require insurers to offer the same products in every state.
C) They affect the types of risks that can be insured and the premiums that can be charged.
D) They eliminate the need for compliance departments within insurance companies.

Correct Answer: C) They affect the types of risks that can be insured and the premiums that can be charged.

Explanation: State-specific regulations play a crucial role in shaping underwriting practices by dictating insurable risks and influencing how premiums are set based on localized factors. Insurers must adapt their products and pricing strategies to comply with each state's regulatory frameworks, addressing diverse risk profiles and consumer protection standards.

Question 14: What is the significance of the Declarations page in an insurance policy?

A) It lists all past claims the policyholder has made.
B) It provides a detailed description of the policy's exclusions.
C) It outlines the fundamental information about the policy, including coverage limits and premium costs.
D) It is only used for health insurance policies.

Correct Answer: C) It outlines the fundamental information about the policy, including coverage limits and premium costs.

Explanation: The Declarations page of an insurance policy is crucial as it summarizes the essential details of the coverage. This includes the insured's name, the policy effective dates, coverage limits, and the premium amounts. This page serves as a quick reference for policyholders to understand what is covered, their responsibilities, and how much they are paying for the coverage.

Question 15: What does the 'Additional Insured' endorsement in a liability insurance policy entail?

A) It extends coverage to other parties not automatically included as insured under the original policy.
B) It increases the premium automatically every year.
C) It covers all employees of the insured as individuals.
D) It reduces the number of claims allowed under the policy.

Correct Answer: A) It extends coverage to other parties not automatically included as insured under the original policy.

Explanation: The 'Additional Insured' endorsement is a common modification made to liability insurance policies. It extends coverage to other parties (such as subcontractors, partners, or landlords) who might otherwise not be covered under the policy but have a potential risk exposure due to their relationship with the primary insured. This endorsement is crucial in business arrangements where multiple parties may face liability risks from the same activities.

Question 16: What is the 'Coinsurance Clause' 's impact on property insurance policies?

A) It ensures all properties are insured to value.
B) It penalizes underinsurance by reducing claim payouts proportionally.
C) It automatically covers new properties acquired by the insured.
D) It guarantees full reimbursement for losses, regardless of the policy limit.

Correct Answer: B) It penalizes underinsurance by reducing claim payouts proportionally.

Explanation: The Coinsurance Clause in property insurance policies is designed to encourage policyholders to insure their properties close to their full value. Suppose the property is insured for less than the stipulated percentage of its actual value (often around 80%). The coinsurance penalty applies in that case, and any claim payout is reduced proportionally. This discourages underinsurance and helps ensure that policyholders carry adequate property coverage.

Question 17: In liability insurance, what role does the 'Duty to Defend' clause play?

A) It obligates the insurer to sue the third party causing the loss.
B) It requires the policyholder to handle all legal defenses themselves.
C) It compels the insurer to manage and finance the defense of claims alleging covered acts.
D) It allows the policyholder to select any attorney they wish without insurer approval.

Correct Answer: C) It compels the insurer to manage and finance the defense of claims alleging covered acts.

Explanation: The 'Duty to Defend' clause is a fundamental aspect of liability insurance policies, where the insurer is obligated to defend the insured against claims that fall within the coverage of the policy. This includes hiring legal counsel and covering the associated legal fees and expenses. This duty is significant as it provides financial relief and support to the insured during legal proceedings.

Question 18: What is the primary benefit of 'Loss Prevention Programs' in the context of workers' compensation insurance?

A) They guarantee a fixed premium for life.
B) They offer discounts on office supplies and equipment.
C) They reduce the likelihood and severity of workplace injuries.
D) They cover all costs of litigation involving employee injuries.

Correct Answer: C) They reduce the likelihood and severity of workplace injuries.

Explanation: Loss Prevention Programs are initiatives undertaken by employers, often in collaboration with their workers' compensation insurers, to reduce the frequency and severity of workplace injuries. These programs may include safety training, ergonomic assessments, and regular safety audits. By preventing accidents, these programs protect employees and help reduce the employer's insurance costs by minimizing claim frequencies and premiums.

Question 19: What is an 'Aggregate Limit' in an insurance policy?

A) The maximum amount the insurer will pay for a single claim.
B) The total amount the insurer will pay for all claims during the policy period.
C) The minimum required limit that all policies must adhere to by law.
D) A temporary increase in coverage limit due to a specific event.

Correct Answer: B) The total amount the insurer will pay for all claims during the policy period.

Explanation: The Aggregate Limit in an insurance policy is the maximum amount an insurer is obligated to pay for all covered losses incurred during a specified policy period. Once this limit is reached, the insurer will no longer cover any additional claims during that period, which emphasizes the importance of understanding coverage limits when choosing a policy.

Question 20: How does the 'Indemnity Principle' operate in insurance?

A) It allows insurers to profit from the policies they write.
B) It ensures that policyholders receive compensation equivalent to their losses, no more, no less.
C) It requires all policyholders to have identical coverage limits.
D) It provides coverage for all possible risks, regardless of the policy terms.

Correct Answer: B) It ensures that policyholders receive compensation equivalent to their losses, no more, no less.

Explanation: The Indemnity Principle is a fundamental concept in insurance that stipulates that insurance policies should compensate the insured for their actual losses, but not more than the loss. This principle prevents policyholders from profiting from their insurance. It maintains the insurer's role as a provider of financial recovery rather than a source of profit.

Question 21: What is the primary benefit of adding a 'Waiver of Subrogation' to a commercial liability policy?

A) It allows the insurer to charge higher premiums.
B) It prevents the insurer from recovering payments made to the insured from a third party.
C) It increases the total coverage limit.
D) It extends the policy to cover additional insured parties.

Correct Answer: B) It prevents the insurer from recovering payments made to the insured from a third party.

Explanation: A 'Waiver of Subrogation' is an endorsement that can be added to insurance policies, where the insurer waives its right to seek compensation from third parties who may have caused an insurance loss to the insured. This is particularly useful in commercial contexts where business relationships might be jeopardized by insurance claims against contractors, clients, or business partners.

Question 22: Under what circumstances would an insurer likely apply a 'Salvage' condition in a property insurance claim?

A) When the insured decides to renew their policy.
B) When the damaged property can be repaired quickly.
C) When the property is a total loss and the insurer takes possession after a payout.
D) When the claim is for a small amount.

Correct Answer: C) When the property is a total loss and the insurer takes possession after a payout.

Explanation: The 'Salvage' condition is used in property insurance when the insurer pays out a total loss claim and then takes possession of the damaged property to recover some of the payout amount by selling the salvageable parts. This process helps mitigate the insurer's financial loss and is an integral part of the property claims process.

Question 23: How does 'Experience Rating' influence workers' compensation insurance premiums?

A) It adjusts premiums based on the global industry performance.
B) It adjusts premiums based solely on the legal jurisdiction.
C) It adjusts premiums based on the insured's past loss experience.
D) It provides a fixed reduction in premiums for all businesses.

Correct Answer: C) It adjusts premiums based on the insured's past loss experience.

Explanation: Experience Rating is a method used in workers' compensation insurance to adjust premiums based on a business's claim history relative to other businesses in the same industry. Companies with fewer claims typically benefit from lower premiums, while those with more claims may see higher rates. This system incentivizes companies to implement safety programs and improve workplace safety.

Question 24: What is the purpose of 'Flood Exclusions' in standard homeowners insurance policies?

A) To provide coverage for all natural disasters without additional premiums.
B) To limit the insurer's liability for damages caused by specific, high-risk events like floods.
C) To ensure that homeowners purchase separate flood insurance policies.
D) To cover minor water damages automatically.

Correct Answer: B) To limit the insurer's liability for damages caused by specific, high-risk events like floods.

Explanation: Flood Exclusions are commonly found in standard homeowners policies to explicitly exclude coverage for damage caused by flooding. These exclusions are necessary because flood risk can be extraordinarily high in certain areas, and managing this risk requires specialized underwriting and pricing that standard policies do not typically provide.

Question 25: What role does 'Proximate Cause' play in determining claims under property and casualty insurance policies?

A) It determines the nearest insurance agent to handle a claim.
B) It identifies the primary reason for the insured event occurring.
C) It is used to calculate the exact amount of damages.
D) It specifies the documentation required for a claim.

Correct Answer: B) It identifies the primary reason for the insured event occurring.

Explanation: Proximate Cause is a key principle in insurance that refers to the primary cause of loss or damage. It is used to determine whether the loss should be covered under the insurance policy terms, based on the initiating event that set off the chain reaction leading to the damage.

Question 26: Why might an insurer require an 'Appraisal' before agreeing to cover a high-value item under a property insurance policy?

A) To determine if the item is within the geographical coverage area.
B) To assess the risk of insuring the item based on its condition and value.
C) To comply with state regulations regarding personal property.
D) To calculate the yearly premiums based on the item's color and style.

Correct Answer: B) To assess the risk of insuring the item based on its condition and value.

Explanation: An appraisal helps the insurer and the insured agree on the value of a high-value item, such as fine art or jewelry, ensuring that the coverage amount reflects its current market value or replacement cost. This is crucial for setting appropriate premiums and limits, and for fair compensation in the event of a claim.

Question 27: What is the significance of 'Agreed Value' in a property insurance policy?

A) It is the amount the insurer agrees to pay regardless of actual costs.
B) It represents a consensus on the amount of premiums paid annually.
C) It is the deductible amount agreed upon at the policy inception.
D) It specifies the terms and conditions of the insurance contract.

Correct Answer: A) It is the amount the insurer agrees to pay regardless of actual costs.

Explanation: The 'Agreed Value' clause in a property insurance policy specifies that the insurer and the insured have agreed upon the value of the property insured at the time the policy is written. This value will be the amount paid out in the event of a total loss, regardless of the actual cash value or replacement cost at the time of the claim. This is particularly important for items whose value might not be easily ascertainable in the market.

Question 28: What typically triggers a 'Business Interruption' insurance claim?

A) A planned closure for renovations.
B) A decrease in market demand for products or services.
C) Direct physical loss or damage to the property that disrupts business operations.
D) Changes in government regulations affecting the industry.

Correct Answer: C) Direct physical loss or damage to the property that disrupts business operations.

Explanation: Business Interruption insurance is designed to cover the loss of income that a business suffers after a disaster while its facility is either closed because of the disaster or in the process of being rebuilt. It is triggered by direct physical damage to the property, such as from a fire or storm, that leads to the cessation of business activities.

Question 29: What is a 'Retroactive Date' in liability insurance policies?

A) The date after which all claims are denied.
B) The date before which claims related to incidents will not be covered.
C) The expiration date of the policy.
D) The date when premium rates are adjusted.

Correct Answer: B) The date before which incidents-related claims will not be covered.

Explanation: The Retroactive Date in a liability insurance policy specifies the earliest point in time when an incident can occur and still be covered by the policy. Any incidents that occur before this date are not covered, which is particularly relevant in claims-made policies where coverage is tied to the policy period in which the claim is made.

Question 30: How do 'Automatic Premium Loans' function in life insurance policies?

A) They allow the insurer to increase the coverage amount automatically.
B) They permit automatic borrowing against the cash value to pay overdue premiums.
C) They automatically convert term insurance to whole-life policies.
D) They enable automatic policy renewal without medical re-examination.

Correct Answer: B) They permit automatic borrowing against the cash value to pay overdue premiums.

Explanation: Automatic Premium Loans are a feature in some life insurance policies that allows the insurer to automatically make a loan against the policy's cash value if the premium is not paid by the end of the grace period. This helps keep the policy in force by using the policy's own value to cover the premiums, thereby preventing accidental lapse due to non-payment.

Question 31: What does an 'Exclusion' in an insurance policy specify?

A) The maximum limit of coverage provided by the policy.
B) Specific conditions or events that are not covered by the policy.
C) The mandatory requirements needed to purchase the policy.
D) The geographic areas where the policy is effective.

Correct Answer: B) Specific conditions or events that are not covered by the policy.

Explanation: Exclusions in an insurance policy are specific conditions, situations, or circumstances that are not covered by the policy. These exclusions are critical for defining the coverage boundaries and are essential for preventing misunderstandings about what the policy will and will not cover. Common exclusions might include events like natural disasters, acts of war, or intentional damage.

Question 32: What is 'Endorsement' in the context of insurance policies?

A) A formal agreement to continue the policy after its expiration.
B) A document altering the terms of the insurance contract.
C) A method for calculating the premium based on the policyholder's credit score.
D) A legal testimony by a third party affirming the validity of the policy.

Correct Answer: B) A document altering the insurance contract terms.

Explanation: An endorsement in an insurance policy is a document that amends or adds to the terms and conditions of the original contract. It can be used to add or remove coverage, and to incorporate any changes agreed upon by the insurer and the insured. This flexibility allows policyholders to adjust their coverage as circumstances change without needing to issue a new policy.

Question 33: Why is 'Risk Assessment' crucial for insurers?

A) It determines the physical health of the company's employees.
B) It assists in setting marketing strategies.
C) It helps insurers set premiums based on the likelihood of a covered event occurring.
D) It is used to determine the geographical location for opening new offices.

Correct Answer: C) It helps insurers set premiums based on the likelihood of a covered event occurring.

Explanation: Risk assessment is a fundamental process in the insurance industry that involves evaluating the potential risks associated with insuring a person or a property. By understanding these risks, insurers can set premiums that are proportionate to the likelihood and potential costs of a covered event. This process ensures financial stability for the insurer and fairness in pricing for policyholders.

Question 34: How do 'Deductibles' influence an insurance policy's premium?

A) Higher deductibles lead to higher premiums.
B) Lower deductibles result in higher premiums.
C) Deductibles are unrelated to premiums.
D) Only variable deductibles affect premiums.

Correct Answer: B) Lower deductibles result in higher premiums.

Explanation: Deductibles are the amount that a policyholder agrees to pay out-of-pocket before the insurance coverage kicks in. Choosing a higher deductible generally leads to lower premiums because the policyholder assumes a greater risk share. Conversely, a lower deductible reduces the risk assumed by the policyholder, resulting in higher premiums.

Question 35: What is the purpose of 'Aggregate Limits' in liability insurance policies?

A) To limit the insurer's exposure to high-cost claims.
B) To increase the coverage limit each year based on inflation.
C) To restrict the number of claims a policyholder can make in one policy term.
D) To extend coverage automatically to new assets acquired during the policy term.

Correct Answer: A) To limit the insurer's exposure to high-cost claims.

Explanation: Aggregate limits in liability insurance policies set a maximum cap on the amount an insurer will pay for all claims during the policy period. This limit helps insurers manage their risk and ensures that they do not face unlimited liability, which could jeopardize their financial stability.

Question 36: Regarding property insurance, what does 'Improvements and Betterments' coverage involve?

A) Coverage for betterments made by tenants that might not be insurable under a standard policy.
B) Insurance for structural improvements mandated by law after a covered loss.
C) Coverage for property enhancements made solely by the insurer.
D) A guarantee that property repairs will use superior materials than those used originally.

Correct Answer: A) Coverage for betterments made by tenants that might not be insurable under a standard policy.

Explanation: 'Improvements and Betterments' refers to upgrades or enhancements made to a leased property by tenants. If these improvements are made at the tenant's expense, they may not be covered under the property owner's policy. This coverage is crucial for tenants to protect their investment in improving the rented space.

Question 37: What is typically covered under 'Special Form' property insurance policies?

A) Only specific risks named in the policy.
B) All risks except those explicitly excluded.
C) Only risks associated with special events or occasions.
D) Risks that are uncommon or unusual.

Correct Answer: B) All risks except those explicitly excluded.

Explanation: Special Form coverage is the most inclusive form of property insurance, offering protection against all perils unless they are specifically excluded in the policy. This broad coverage ensures that policyholders are protected against a wide range of potential risks, providing greater security and peace of mind.

Question 38: What does the term 'Umbrella Policy' refer to in insurance?

A) A policy that provides additional coverage for items typically not covered by standard policies.
B) A policy that combines various types of insurance into one package.
C) A supplemental policy that provides extra liability coverage above the limits of an underlying policy.
D) A policy designed for businesses operating in multiple industries.

Correct Answer: C) A supplemental policy that provides extra liability coverage above the limits of an underlying policy.

Explanation: An Umbrella Policy offers additional liability coverage beyond the limits of the insured's homeowners, auto, or watercraft policies. It helps protect against potentially ruinous liability claims or judgments, filling in gaps in coverage and providing an added layer of security.

Question 39: How does 'Inflation Guard' endorsements impact property insurance policies?

A) They decrease the policy premium based on inflation rates.
B) They automatically adjust the coverage limits based on inflationary trends to maintain adequate coverage.
C) They eliminate the need for annual policy reviews.
D) They provide discounts on premiums when inflation rates are high.

Correct Answer: B) They automatically adjust the coverage limits based on inflationary trends to maintain adequate coverage.

Explanation: Inflation Guard endorsements are important in property insurance as they ensure the coverage limits keep pace with inflation. This automatic adjustment helps maintain sufficient coverage amounts to replace or repair the insured property in today's dollars, accounting for rising costs due to inflation.

Question 40: What does 'Loss Payable Clause' in a commercial property policy signify?

A) A clause that defines how losses are calculated and paid.
B) A provision that specifies a third party who may receive payment in the event of a claim.
C) A clause that dictates the timeline for paying out claims.
D) A requirement for the insured to pay a portion of the loss before the insurer pays the remainder.

Correct Answer: B) A provision that specifies a third party who may receive payment in the event of a claim.

Explanation: The Loss Payable Clause is used in commercial property policies to designate a party other than the insured who may receive the insurance proceeds directly. This is often used when a third party, such as a lender or lessor, has a financial interest in the insured property. It ensures that the interests of all parties with a stake in the property are protected in the event of a loss.

Question 41: What is 'Insurance Adjusters' primary role in the claims process?

A) To determine the premium rates for policy renewals.
B) To negotiate policy sales to new clients.
C) To assess the validity and value of a claim filed by an insured.
D) To provide legal representation for insurance companies in court.

Correct Answer: C) To assess the validity and value of a claim filed by an insured.

Explanation: Insurance Adjusters play a critical role in the claims handling process. Their primary responsibility is to investigate claims, assess damage, determine the insurer's liability, and help ensure that claims are settled fairly. They review the circumstances of the claim, inspect any damaged property, interview witnesses, and gather information to make a balanced decision on the claim.

Question 42: How does 'Liquor Liability Insurance' differ from general liability policies in its coverage?

A) It covers only internal corporate events where liquor is served.
B) It covers explicitly damages caused by individuals under the influence of alcohol served by the policyholder's business.
C) It extends to any alcohol consumption incident on the business premises.
D) It provides coverage for manufacturing alcoholic beverages.

Correct Answer: B) It specifically covers damages caused by individuals under the influence of alcohol the policyholder's business serves.

Explanation: Liquor Liability Insurance is essential for businesses that manufacture, sell, or serve alcoholic beverages. It covers the business against claims resulting from damages or injuries caused by intoxicated patrons. This type of insurance is critical due to the potential for significant legal liabilities arising from alcohol-related incidents, which are not typically covered under general liability policies.

Question 43: What is the 'Return Premium' in insurance terms?

A) A reward system for claim-free years.
B) An additional premium charged for extending coverage mid-term.
C) The portion of the premium returned to the insured when the policy is canceled.
D) Interest earned on paid premiums.

Correct Answer: C) The portion of the premium returned to the insured when the policy is canceled.

Explanation: The Return Premium occurs when a policy is terminated prior to its expiration date, and the insurer returns the unused portion of the paid premium to the policyholder. This situation might arise if the risk insured against has been eliminated or significantly reduced, or if the policyholder chooses to cancel the policy for other reasons.

Question 44: How do 'Surety Bonds' function within the context of insurance?

A) They insure property against theft and vandalism.
B) They guarantee the repayment of loans and debts.
C) They ensure the completion of contractual obligations by a third party.
D) They cover medical expenses for workplace injuries.

Correct Answer: C) They ensure the completion of contractual obligations by a third party.

Explanation: Surety Bonds are a form of financial guarantee insurance where the surety (insurance company) guarantees the obligee (the project owner) that the principal (the contractor) will fulfill their contractual obligations. Suppose the principal fails to meet their obligations. In that case, the surety covers the resulting financial loss up to the bond limit, and then seeks reimbursement from the principal.

Question 45: What is typically covered under 'Garage Keepers Insurance'?

A) Customer vehicles in a repair shop's custody.
B) The personal vehicles of employees at a business.
C) Any vehicle parked in a commercial parking garage.
D) Theft of tools from a garage.

Correct Answer: A) Customer vehicles in a repair shop's custody.

Explanation: Garage Keepers Insurance is a specialized type of coverage designed to protect auto service businesses from liability when customers' vehicles are damaged while being repaired, serviced, or stored in the facility. This insurance is crucial for mitigating financial risks associated with potential damages or losses to vehicles under the care of the business.

Question 46: What is the key function of 'Business Owners Policy (BOP)' in commercial insurance?

A) To provide bundled property and liability protection for small business owners.
B) To insure business owners against personal liability claims.
C) To cover the health benefits of employees.
D) To protect against data breaches and cyber threats.

Correct Answer: A) To provide bundled property and liability protection for small business owners.

Explanation: A Business Owners Policy (BOP) is designed to offer a combination of coverage options that protect small to medium-sized businesses against property damage, liability risks, and business interruption losses. This bundled policy simplifies the insurance buying process and can be customized to meet specific business needs, making it a cost-effective and comprehensive insurance solution for business owners.

Question 47: What does 'Consequential Loss' refer to in the context of property insurance?

A) Direct damage to property due to natural disasters.
B) Losses as a direct consequence of theft or burglary.
C) Financial losses resulting indirectly from a covered event.
D) Legal liabilities resulting from property damage.

Correct Answer: C) Financial losses resulting indirectly from a covered event.

Explanation: Consequential Loss, also known as business interruption loss, refers to the financial impact suffered due to inability to conduct business normally due to damage to property. This includes losses like lost revenue, extra expenses incurred to maintain operations, and other financial challenges that are not directly caused by physical damage but are the consequence of it.

Question 48: What is 'Contingent Business Interruption' insurance designed to cover?

A) Losses from interruption due to a supplier's failure to deliver goods.
B) Direct damage to business premises and assets.
C) Employee salaries during periods of business closure.
D) Costs associated with relocating a business.

Correct Answer: A) Losses from interruption due to a supplier's failure to deliver goods.

Explanation: Contingent Business Interruption insurance provides coverage for financial losses that occur when a key supplier or partner experiences a disruption that directly affects the insured's business operations. This type of insurance is crucial for companies that rely heavily on external suppliers for materials or products.

Question 49: How does 'Employment Practices Liability Insurance (EPLI)' protect businesses?

A) Covers damages from employee claims regarding wrongful termination, discrimination, and harassment.
B) Insures against injuries that occur to employees on the job.
C) Protects against claims of improper employee management.
D) Provides coverage for theft or embezzlement by employees.

Correct Answer: A) Covers damages from employee claims regarding wrongful termination, discrimination, and harassment.

Explanation: Employment Practices Liability Insurance (EPLI) is designed to protect employers from the financial fallout of litigation resulting from employment-related claims. This includes allegations of wrongful termination, discrimination, workplace harassment, and other violations of employee rights. EPLI is increasingly important in a litigious society where such claims can be financially draining and damaging to a company's reputation.

Question 50: What role does 'Loss Ratio' play in the insurance industry?

A) It measures the profitability of an insurance company by comparing claims paid to premiums received.
B) It determines the maximum coverage limit for high-risk policies.
C) It calculates the premiums based on the geographic location of the insured.
D) It assesses the environmental impact of insurance policies.

Correct Answer: A) It measures the profitability of an insurance company by comparing claims paid to premiums received.

Explanation: The Loss Ratio is a critical financial metric in the insurance industry that helps assess an insurer's profitability. It is calculated by dividing the total amount of claims paid (including adjustment expenses) by the total premium income received. A high loss ratio indicates that the insurer is paying out almost as much, or more, in claims as it is receiving from premiums, which could signal financial instability or pricing issues.

CALIFORNIA QUESTIONS

(Go to the last page of the book to download all the 1000+ state-specific questions)

Question 1:
In California, what is the minimum liability coverage required under a standard auto insurance policy?

A) $10,000 for bodily injury per person
B) $15,000 for bodily injury per person
C) $25,000 for bodily injury per person
D) $30,000 for bodily injury per person

Correct Answer:
B) $15,000 for bodily injury per person

Explanation:
California law requires that all drivers carry a minimum of $15,000 for bodily injury liability per person, $30,000 for bodily injury liability per accident, and $5,000 for property damage liability (commonly referred to as 15/30/5 coverage).

Question 2:
Which agency regulates the insurance industry in California?

A) California Department of Insurance
B) California State Treasury
C) California Financial Services Authority
D) California Bureau of Consumer Affairs

Correct Answer:
A) California Department of Insurance

Explanation:
The California Department of Insurance is responsible for regulating the insurance industry in California, overseeing the enforcement of the state's insurance laws and regulations.

Question 3:
What is the purpose of the California FAIR Plan?

A) To provide auto insurance to high-risk drivers
B) To offer health insurance subsidies to low-income families
C) To provide basic fire insurance coverage to homeowners in high-risk areas
D) To regulate the financial operations of insurance companies

Correct Answer:
C) To provide basic fire insurance coverage to homeowners in high-risk areas

Explanation:
The California FAIR Plan is an insurance pool established to assure that basic fire insurance coverage is available to homeowners situated in areas of California that are prone to wildfires and where traditional insurance may be hard to obtain.

Question 4:
Under California law, what is one of the required provisions that must be included in every insurance policy?

A) A mandatory arbitration clause
B) A clause waiving the insurer's right to subrogation
C) A provision for the appraisal of losses
D) An automatic renewal clause

Correct Answer:
C) A provision for the appraisal of losses

Explanation:
California insurance law requires that every insurance policy must include a provision for the appraisal of losses if there is a disagreement between the insurer and the insured on the value of the claim.

Question 5:
What does California's Proposition 103 regulate?

A) The process for electing the Insurance Commissioner
B) Premium rates for residential and auto insurance policies
C) Licensing requirements for insurance agents
D) The establishment of new insurance companies in the state

Correct Answer:
B) Premium rates for residential and auto insurance policies

Explanation:
Proposition 103, passed in 1988, requires that insurance companies in California roll back and then freeze their rates for residential and auto insurance until the state approves any future increases. It significantly impacts how insurance rates are set and adjusted in California.

Question 6:
In California, what is the minimum number of competitive quotes an insurance agent must obtain before placing coverage with the California FAIR Plan?

A) One
B) Two
C) Three
D) Four

Correct Answer:
C) Three

Explanation:
California law requires that before placing coverage with the California FAIR Plan, an insurance agent must obtain a minimum of three competitive quotes to ensure that the FAIR Plan is used as a last resort.

Question 7:
Which type of bond is mandatory for all public insurance adjusters operating in California?

A) Performance bond
B) Fidelity bond
C) Surety bond
D) Contract bond

Correct Answer:
C) Surety bond

Explanation:
All public insurance adjusters in California are required to have a surety bond in place before they can be licensed to operate. This bond provides a level of protection to consumers by ensuring that adjusters adhere to applicable laws and regulations.

Question 8:
What action must insurers take when renewing a homeowner's insurance policy in California?

A) Offer a new policy with identical coverage at the same premium
B) Provide the policyholder with a comparison of the old and new rates and coverages
C) Automatically renew the policy without notifying the policyholder
D) Obtain a new application from the policyholder

Correct Answer:
B) Provide the policyholder with a comparison of the old and new rates and coverages

Explanation:
Upon renewal of a homeowner's insurance policy in California, insurers are required to provide the policyholder with a clear comparison of the old and new rates and coverages, helping consumers make informed decisions about their insurance needs.

Question 9:
In California, how are insurance rates primarily determined?

A) By the California Department of Insurance after public hearings
B) By each insurance company, but must be approved by the California Department of Insurance
C) Solely based on the national average
D) By the Governor's office directly

Correct Answer:
B) By each insurance company, but must be approved by the California Department of Insurance

Explanation:
In California, insurance companies propose their own rates, but these must be approved by the California Department of Insurance. This process ensures rates are adequate, not excessive, and not unfairly discriminatory.

Question 10:
What unique provision does California law include regarding auto insurance coverage for newly acquired vehicles?

A) Immediate coverage is provided for any new vehicle purchased by the policyholder for the first 30 days.
B) No coverage is provided until the new vehicle is reported to the insurer.
C) Coverage for a newly acquired vehicle is only provided if it replaces a vehicle already listed on the policy.

D) Only theft coverage is automatically provided for newly purchased vehicles.

Correct Answer:
A) Immediate coverage is provided for any new vehicle purchased by the policyholder for the first 30 days.

Explanation:
California auto insurance policies automatically cover any new vehicle acquired by the policyholder for the first 30 days following the purchase, giving the policyholder time to formally add the new vehicle to their policy without a lapse in coverage.

Question 11:
Which California law requires insurers to act in good faith and deal fairly with policyholders, prohibiting deceptive practices?

A) California Fair Access to Insurance Requirements (FAIR) Act
B) California Insurance Equality Act
C) California Unfair Practices Act
D) California Consumer Protection Act

Correct Answer:
C) California Unfair Practices Act

Explanation:
The California Unfair Practices Act requires insurers to act in good faith and deal fairly with all policyholders, explicitly prohibiting deceptive, misleading, or otherwise unfair practices in the insurance industry.

Question 12:
What is required under California law for a homeowner's insurance policy when insuring against the peril of fire?

A) A separate fire insurance policy must be purchased.
B) Fire coverage must be included in all standard homeowners policies.
C) Only homes in urban areas must include fire coverage.
D) Homeowners in wildfire-prone areas are exempt from mandatory fire insurance.
Correct Answer:
B) Fire coverage must be included in all standard homeowners policies.

Explanation:
Under California law, coverage against the peril of fire is mandatory and must be included in all standard homeowners insurance policies, providing critical protection given the state's high risk of wildfires.

Question 13:
In the context of California auto insurance, what is "Medical Payments Coverage"?

A) Coverage that pays for medical expenses of the policyholder only in a no-fault accident.
B) Coverage that pays for medical expenses regardless of fault in an accident.
C) Coverage that only pays for medical expenses exceeding the policyholder's health insurance limits.
D) Mandatory coverage for all vehicle policies.

Correct Answer:
B) Coverage that pays for medical expenses regardless of fault in an accident.

Explanation:
Medical Payments Coverage in California auto insurance policies covers medical expenses for the policyholder and passengers, regardless of who is at fault in an accident, ensuring timely medical attention without the need for litigation.

Question 14:
What does the California "Consent to Rate" form signify?

A) The policyholder agrees to rates higher than those approved by the state.
B) The policyholder agrees to automatically renew their policy.
C) The insurer agrees to lower rates upon the policyholder's request.
D) The policyholder consents to receive all communications electronically.

Correct Answer:
A) The policyholder agrees to rates higher than those approved by the state.

Explanation:
A "Consent to Rate" form in California is used when an insurer needs to charge rates higher than those typically approved by the state. The policyholder must agree to these rates explicitly, ensuring transparency and consent in premium pricing.

Question 15:
How does California address the issue of uninsured motorists?

A) By offering state-funded insurance for low-income drivers.

B) Through strict penalties including fines and vehicle impoundment.
C) By requiring all drivers to carry uninsured motorist coverage.
D) All motorists are assumed to have insurance through their vehicle registration.

Correct Answer:
B) Through strict penalties including fines and vehicle impoundment.

Explanation:
California addresses the issue of uninsured motorists through enforcement measures including fines, vehicle impoundment, and license suspension, aiming to ensure all drivers maintain at least the minimum required insurance coverage.

Question 16:
What is the primary function of the California Earthquake Authority (CEA)?

A) To regulate building codes and standards in earthquake-prone areas.
B) To provide earthquake insurance to homeowners who might otherwise be unable to obtain it.
C) To oversee all seismic activity monitoring within the state.
D) To fund and conduct research on earthquake preparedness.

Correct Answer:
B) To provide earthquake insurance to homeowners who might otherwise be unable to obtain it.

Explanation:
The California Earthquake Authority (CEA) offers earthquake insurance policies to California homeowners, providing a crucial option for financial protection against earthquakes, which are not covered under standard homeowners insurance policies.

Question 17:
Under what condition can a California insurer legally refuse to renew an auto insurance policy?

A) The driver has received one speeding ticket.
B) The vehicle is over 10 years old.
C) The policyholder has moved to a different state.
D) The policyholder has not submitted feedback on customer service.

Correct Answer:
C) The policyholder has moved to a different state.

Explanation:
In California, an insurer can legally refuse to renew an auto insurance policy if the policyholder has moved to a different state, as the policy must comply with the insurance laws and requirements of the policyholder's new state of residence.

Question 18:
What is the primary use of "Agreed Value" insurance policies in California?

A) For coverage of standard automobile losses
B) For life insurance agreements
C) For insuring valuable items like artworks and collectibles
D) For health insurance contracts

Correct Answer:
C) For insuring valuable items like artworks and collectibles

Explanation:
In California, "Agreed Value" insurance policies are particularly useful for insuring high-value items such as artworks, collectibles, and antiques. These policies allow the insurer and the policyholder to agree upon the value of the insured item at the inception of the policy, ensuring that the policyholder receives a predefined payout amount in the event of a loss, which helps avoid disputes over the value of the item after a claim is made.

Question 19:
How does California law ensure transparency in the calculation of auto insurance premiums?

A) By requiring insurers to publicly post their premium formulas
B) By mandating a state review and approval of all premium changes
C) By allowing policyholders to request detailed premium calculations
D) By conducting annual public hearings on auto insurance rates

Correct Answer:
B) By mandating a state review and approval of all premium changes

Explanation:
California law ensures transparency in auto insurance premiums by requiring that all changes to premium rates be submitted for state review and approval. This process helps prevent unjustified premium increases and protects consumers from arbitrary rate hikes.

Question 20:
What must California insurers provide to claimants during the auto insurance claim process?

A) A rental car for the duration of the vehicle repair
B) A written estimate of the claim payout within 10 days of claim filing
C) Regular updates every five days until the claim is resolved
D) A detailed explanation of the claim denial if the claim is not approved

Correct Answer:
D) A detailed explanation of the claim denial if the claim is not approved

Explanation:
California law requires insurers to provide a detailed explanation of the reasons for a claim denial if an auto insurance claim is not approved. This requirement is part of the state's efforts to ensure fairness and transparency in the claims handling process.

Question 21:
What specific legislation in California requires commercial properties to have earthquake coverage?

A) The California Seismic Safety Act
B) The Mandatory Earthquake Coverage Law
C) No specific legislation mandates earthquake coverage for commercial properties
D) The California Earthquake Authority Act

Correct Answer:
C) No specific legislation mandates earthquake coverage for commercial properties

Explanation:
In California, there is no specific legislation that mandates earthquake coverage for commercial properties. Owners of commercial properties must decide whether to purchase earthquake coverage based on their assessment of risk and the recommendations of their insurance provider.

Question 22:
In the event of an auto accident in California, what is the minimum property damage liability coverage required by law?

A) $5,000
B) $10,000
C) $15,000
D) $20,000

Correct Answer:
A) $5,000

Explanation:
California law requires a minimum of $5,000 in property damage liability coverage for auto insurance. This coverage helps pay for damage the policyholder might cause to someone else's property during an automobile accident.

Question 23:
What is the primary role of the California Insurance Guarantee Association?

A) To invest in insurance companies to ensure market stability
B) To act as a reinsurance carrier for insurance companies operating in California
C) To provide protection to insureds if their insurance company becomes insolvent
D) To license new insurance companies within the state

Correct Answer:
C) To provide protection to insureds if their insurance company becomes insolvent

Explanation:
The California Insurance Guarantee Association provides a safety net for policyholders whose insurance companies become insolvent. It ensures that covered claims are paid up to a specified limit, protecting consumers from loss due to insurer insolvency.

Question 24:
How often must a licensed insurance agent in California complete ethics training as part of their continuing education requirements?

A) Every year
B) Every two years
C) Every three years
D) Every four years

Correct Answer:
B) Every two years

Explanation:
In California, licensed insurance agents are required to complete ethics training as part of their continuing education every two years. This requirement helps ensure that agents remain aware of ethical standards and practices relevant to their profession.

Question 25:
What provision does California law include regarding the timely communication of claim decisions by insurers?

A) Decisions must be communicated within 10 days of receiving proof of claim
B) Decisions must be communicated within 15 days of receiving proof of claim
C) Decisions must be communicated within 30 days of receiving proof of claim
D) Decisions must be communicated within 40 days of receiving proof of claim

Correct Answer:
D) Decisions must be communicated within 40 days of receiving proof of claim

Explanation:
California law requires that insurers communicate decisions regarding claims within 40 days after receiving proof of claim. This provision is intended to ensure timely processing and prevent undue delays that can negatively affect claimants.

Question 26:
Which type of coverage is compulsory for all new cars purchased with a loan in California?

A) Liability insurance
B) Comprehensive insurance
C) Collision insurance
D) Personal Injury Protection (PIP)

Correct Answer:
C) Collision insurance

Explanation:
In California, collision insurance is compulsory for all new cars purchased with a loan. This requirement is often stipulated by lenders to protect the investment in the vehicle until the loan is paid off.

Question 27:
What is the Consumer Bill of Rights concerning insurance in California?

A) A document that outlines the rights of insurance companies
B) A legislative act that must be voted on bi-annually
C) A set of guidelines that insurance companies must follow to ensure fair treatment of consumers
D) A form that consumers must sign before purchasing insurance

Correct Answer:
C) A set of guidelines that insurance companies must follow to ensure fair treatment of consumers

Explanation:
The Consumer Bill of Rights in California is a set of guidelines that insurance companies must adhere to, ensuring that consumers are treated fairly and ethically. It covers aspects such as timely payment of claims, the right to privacy, and fair underwriting practices.

Question 28:
In California, what is the penalty for an insurance agent who is found guilty of coercion or misleading a client?

A) A fine of up to $10,000
B) License suspension for up to one year
C) Both a fine and license suspension
D) Mandatory retraining in ethics

Correct Answer:
C) Both a fine and license suspension

Explanation:
In California, an insurance agent found guilty of coercion or misleading a client can face both a fine and a suspension of their license. These penalties serve as deterrents to unethical behavior and protect consumers.

Question 29:
What does the term 'admitted insurer' refer to in California?

A) An insurer that has been formally admitted to the California insurance market by the Department of Insurance
B) An insurer that is allowed to admit mistakes without penalties
C) An insurer that primarily admits claims without investigation
D) An insurer that has admitted to past regulatory violations but is still allowed to operate

Correct Answer:
A) An insurer that has been formally admitted to the California insurance market by the Department of Insurance

Explanation:
An 'admitted insurer' in California is an insurance company that has received formal approval from the California Department of Insurance to transact business in the state. This status also means the insurer

must comply with all state regulations and contributes to the California Insurance Guarantee Association.

Question 30:
How is the insurance commissioner selected in California?

A) Appointed by the governor
B) Elected by the public in statewide elections
C) Chosen by the state legislature
D) Appointed by the California Department of Insurance

Correct Answer:
B) Elected by the public in statewide elections

Explanation:
The insurance commissioner in California is elected by the public in statewide elections. This position is responsible for overseeing the function and regulation of the insurance industry within the state.

Question 31:
What does the California Proposition 103 require insurers to primarily base their rates on?

A) The client's age and gender
B) The location of the client's residence
C) The client's credit score
D) The client's driving record, miles driven per year, and years of driving experience

Correct Answer:
D) The client's driving record, miles driven per year, and years of driving experience

Explanation:
Proposition 103 in California requires that auto insurance rates be primarily based on factors directly related to the risk of accident, such as the driver's record, miles driven per year, and years of driving experience, rather than personal characteristics.

Question 32:
In California, what legal document must be filed by an insurer to initiate the subrogation process after paying a claim?

A) A Notice of Subrogation
B) A Subrogation Waiver

C) A Subrogation Demand
D) A Claims Settlement

Correct Answer:
A) A Notice of Subrogation

Explanation:
In California, an insurer must file a Notice of Subrogation to formally initiate the subrogation process. This notice is used to inform the party responsible for the loss that the insurer intends to pursue recovery of the amounts paid on the claim.

Question 33:
How are surplus line brokers regulated in California?

A) They are not required to hold any specific license
B) They must hold a special surplus line license
C) They operate under a general property and casualty license
D) They are regulated by the federal government

Correct Answer:
B) They must hold a special surplus line license

Explanation:
Surplus line brokers in California must hold a special surplus line license, which allows them to place coverage with non-admitted insurers when coverage cannot be placed with admitted insurers.

Question 34:
What is the primary purpose of the California Insurance Code Section 790.03, also known as the Unfair Practices Act?

A) To define and regulate ethical practices in the sale of securities
B) To outline acceptable marketing practices in the insurance industry
C) To prohibit and penalize unfair practices in the insurance business
D) To establish guidelines for environmental liability coverage

Correct Answer:
C) To prohibit and penalize unfair practices in the insurance business

Explanation:

California Insurance Code Section 790.03, also known as the Unfair Practices Act, aims to prohibit and penalize unfair or deceptive acts or practices in the insurance business, including misrepresentation and false advertising of insurance policies.

Question 35:
Under what circumstances can an insurance policy be legally cancelled by the insurer in California once it has been in effect for 60 days or more?

A) Only for non-payment of premium, fraud, or material misrepresentation
B) At the discretion of the insurer with no required reason
C) For any reason but with a 90-day notice
D) Only if both the insurer and insured agree to cancel

Correct Answer:
A) Only for non-payment of premium, fraud, or material misrepresentation

Explanation:
In California, once an insurance policy has been in effect for 60 days or more, it can only be cancelled by the insurer for specific reasons such as non-payment of premium, the commission of fraud by the insured, or material misrepresentation by the insured.

Question 36:
What is required for a vehicle to be classified as "salvage" in California?

A) The vehicle must be over 10 years old
B) The vehicle has been stolen and not recovered within 30 days
C) The cost to repair the vehicle exceeds its insured value
D) The vehicle has been involved in a flood

Correct Answer:
C) The cost to repair the vehicle exceeds its insured value

Explanation:
In California, a vehicle is classified as "salvage" when the cost to repair the vehicle exceeds its insured value. This typically occurs after a major accident or other significant damage.

Question 37:
What is the main function of the California Life and Health Insurance Guarantee Association?

A) To promote life and health insurance products

B) To set premiums for life and health insurance policies
C) To protect policyholders if an insurer becomes insolvent
D) To provide educational resources about life and health insurance

Correct Answer:
C) To protect policyholders if an insurer becomes insolvent

Explanation:
The California Life and Health Insurance Guarantee Association protects policyholders, within limits, against the failure of an insolvent insurer to perform contractual obligations due to insolvency.

Question 38:
What must insurers do to comply with California's mandatory offer of earthquake coverage?

A) Offer earthquake coverage as part of all property insurance policies
B) Offer earthquake coverage as a separate policy at least every two years
C) Include automatic earthquake coverage in all new policies
D) Provide discounts for earthquake retrofits on insured properties

Correct Answer:
B) Offer earthquake coverage as a separate policy at least every two years

Explanation:
California law requires insurers that sell residential property insurance to offer earthquake coverage as a separate policy at least every two years. This requirement ensures that homeowners have the opportunity to purchase earthquake insurance regularly.

Question 39:
How does California define a "good driver" under the Good Driver Discount Policy?

A) A driver with no moving violations in three years
B) A driver with one or fewer points on their driving record in the past three years
C) A driver who has completed a defensive driving course
D) A driver with no at-fault accidents in five years

Correct Answer:
B) A driver with one or fewer points on their driving record in the past three years

Explanation:

Under the Good Driver Discount Policy, California defines a "good driver" as someone who has not had more than one point on their driving record due to a moving violation within the past three years.

Question 40:
What is a "twisting" violation in the context of California insurance law?

A) Changing policy terms without notifying the policyholder
B) Misrepresenting the terms of an existing policy to induce cancellation and purchase of a new policy
C) Failing to submit premium payments collected from clients
D) Unauthorized trading of company insurance funds

Correct Answer:

B) Misrepresenting the terms of an existing policy to induce cancellation and purchase of a new policy

Explanation:

"Twisting" in California insurance law refers to the practice of misrepresenting the terms of an existing insurance policy to persuade a policyholder to cancel it and purchase a new one, often to the detriment of the policyholder.

Question 41:
What unique aspect of California insurance law affects underwriting and pricing of auto insurance policies?

A) Credit scores may be used.
B) Gender may be considered.
C) The insured's occupation may be considered.
D) ZIP codes cannot be the primary factor.

Correct Answer: D) ZIP codes cannot be the primary factor.

Explanation:
In California, ZIP codes cannot be used as the primary factor in determining the rates for auto insurance, ensuring rates are more equitable across different geographic locations.

Question 42:
In California, what happens if an insurance company is found to be in violation of fair claims handling regulations?

A) A fine is imposed for each violation
B) Immediate license suspension
C) Mandatory retraining of staff
D) All of the above

Correct Answer: D) All of the above

Explanation:
California regulators may impose fines, suspend licenses, and require retraining of staff if an insurance company is found to be in violation of fair claims handling regulations, ensuring strict adherence to legal standards.

Question 43:
In the context of California insurance, what is a "Twisting"?

A) Refusing to renew a policy for no valid reason.
B) Making misleading comparisons to persuade a policyholder to switch policies.
C) Charging premiums more frequently than annually.
D) Failing to disclose policy limits to policyholders.

Correct Answer: B) Making misleading comparisons to persuade a policyholder to switch policies.

Explanation:
Twisting in insurance is an unethical practice where an agent makes misleading comparisons of different policies to convince a customer to switch from one policy to another, often to the detriment of the policyholder.

Question 44:
What specific action is required for California insurance agents when changing companies they represent?

A) Notify the California Department of Insurance within 30 days.
B) There is no specific action required as long as the agent remains licensed.
C) Obtain a new license for each company represented.
D) Update their agent profile on the California Department of Insurance website.

Correct Answer: D) Update their agent profile on the California Department of Insurance website.

Explanation:
California requires insurance agents to keep their employment information current, which includes updating their profile on the California Department of Insurance website whenever they change the companies they represent.

Question 45:
What are the record-keeping requirements for insurance agents in California?

A) Maintain records for five years.
B) Keep records for the duration of the policy term plus three years.
C) Store records for at least ten years after a policy expires.
D) No specific record-keeping requirements are mandated.

Correct Answer: B) Keep records for the duration of the policy term plus three years.

Explanation:
California requires insurance agents to keep all policy-related records for the duration of the policy term plus an additional three years to ensure transparency and accountability.

Question 46:
What does the California Guarantee Association do?

A) Provides loans to small insurance companies.
B) Acts as a reinsurance fund for natural disasters.
C) Protects policyholders if their insurance company becomes insolvent.
D) Guarantees the accuracy of insurance company advertising.

Correct Answer: C) Protects policyholders if their insurance company becomes insolvent.

Explanation:
The California Guarantee Association protects policyholders by covering claims if their insurance company becomes insolvent, ensuring that covered losses are paid despite the insurer's financial failure.

Question 47:
How is arbitration used in the resolution of California insurance disputes?

A) Arbitration is mandatory for all insurance disputes.
B) Arbitration can be chosen if both parties agree after the dispute arises.

C) Arbitration is used only for commercial insurance disputes.
D) California does not allow arbitration for insurance disputes.

Correct Answer: B) Arbitration can be chosen if both parties agree after the dispute arises.

Explanation:
In California, arbitration is an option for resolving insurance disputes but only if both parties agree to it after the dispute has arisen. This provides a flexible and potentially faster alternative to court proceedings.

Question 48:
What does the term "binding authority" refer to in California insurance practice?

A) The legal power of an agent to issue a policy on behalf of an insurer.
B) The obligation of a policyholder to comply with policy terms.
C) A mandatory arbitration clause in any insurance contract.
D) The insurer's commitment to abide by state regulations.

Correct Answer: A) The legal power of an agent to issue a policy on behalf of an insurer.

Explanation:
In California insurance practice, "binding authority" refers to the legal power granted to an agent or broker to enter into insurance contracts on behalf of an insurer, making the contracts valid and enforceable.

Question 49:
What specific role does the California Insurance Code play in regulating policy cancellations?

A) It prohibits all cancellations except for non-payment of premium.
B) It outlines acceptable reasons for cancellation and requires proper notice.
C) It allows insurers to cancel policies at any time without reason.
D) It focuses solely on auto insurance policy cancellations.

Correct Answer: B) It outlines acceptable reasons for cancellation and requires proper notice.

Explanation:
The California Insurance Code specifies acceptable reasons for an insurer to cancel a policy and mandates that proper notice be given to the policyholder, ensuring fair treatment and time to find alternative coverage.

Question 50:
What are the requirements for electronic signatures on insurance documents in California?

A) Electronic signatures are not recognized.
B) Recognized if verified through a certified digital platform.
C) Accepted on all insurance documents without additional requirements.
D) Only accepted for non-binding documents.

Correct Answer: B) Recognized if verified through a certified digital platform.

Explanation:
In California, electronic signatures on insurance documents are recognized and legally binding if they are verified through a certified digital platform, facilitating the use of digital transactions in the insurance industry.

Question 51:
What is required under California law regarding the disclosure of insurance broker fees?

A) Broker fees do not need to be disclosed.
B) Broker fees must be disclosed in writing before the purchase of a policy.
C) Disclosure of broker fees is only required when exceeding $100.
D) Broker fees are included in the premium and do not need separate disclosure.

Correct Answer: B) Broker fees must be disclosed in writing before the purchase of a policy.

Explanation:
California law requires that all broker fees be clearly disclosed in writing to the client before the purchase of any insurance policy, ensuring transparency and informed consent from the consumer.

Question 52:
How does California protect consumers with the "Notice of Privacy Practices"?

A) By restricting the sharing of medical information without consent.
B) Consumers have the right to request the correction of their personal information.
C) Both A and B.
D) There are no specific privacy practices required in California.

Correct Answer: C) Both A and B.

Explanation:
California ensures consumer protection with the "Notice of Privacy Practices" by restricting the sharing of medical and personal information without explicit consent and granting consumers the right to request corrections to their personal information.

Question 53:
What is the California DOI's role in consumer complaints against insurers?

A) To provide legal representation to consumers in disputes.
B) To mediate disputes between consumers and insurers.
C) To automatically side with the consumer in disputes.
D) Only to record complaints without further action.

Correct Answer: B) To mediate disputes between consumers and insurers.

Explanation:
The California Department of Insurance (DOI) mediates disputes between consumers and insurers, providing a platform for resolution and ensuring fair handling of complaints.

Question 54:
What stipulations are there for advertising life insurance in California?

A) Advertisements must provide examples of all potential outcomes.
B) Advertisements cannot include estimations of future dividends.
C) Advertisements must be approved by the California DOI.
D) Life insurance advertisements must guarantee policy approval.

Correct Answer: B) Advertisements cannot include estimations of future dividends.

Explanation:
In California, life insurance advertisements are strictly regulated to prevent misleading information, including a prohibition on including estimations of future dividends which cannot be guaranteed.

Question 55:
What mandatory provision must California health insurers include regarding maternity services?

A) Coverage for maternity services is optional.
B) Maternity services must be covered from the date of policy inception.

C) Maternity services are covered only if additional premiums are paid.
D) Coverage for maternity services must be equal to other medical conditions.

Correct Answer: D) Coverage for maternity services must be equal to other medical conditions.

Explanation:
California law mandates that health insurers provide coverage for maternity services and that such coverage must be on par with the coverage provided for other medical conditions.

Question 56:
How are salvage vehicles regulated under California insurance law?

A) Salvage vehicles cannot be insured.
B) Insurers must provide full coverage for salvage vehicles.
C) Salvage titles must be clearly disclosed in any sale.
D) There are no specific regulations for salvage vehicles.

Correct Answer: C) Salvage titles must be clearly disclosed in any sale.

Explanation:
California requires that any vehicle with a salvage title—typically vehicles that have been significantly damaged—must be clearly disclosed as such during any sale, ensuring transparency and informed buying decisions.

Question 57:
Under California law, how are insurance premiums affected by the use of non-original equipment manufacturer (non-OEM) parts in auto repairs?

A) Use of non-OEM parts leads to higher premiums.
B) Premiums cannot be influenced by the use of non-OEM parts.
C) Premiums are reduced if non-OEM parts are used.
D) Insurers must disclose if non-OEM parts are used in repairs.

Correct Answer: D) Insurers must disclose if non-OEM parts are used in repairs.

Explanation:
In California, while the use of non-OEM parts does not directly affect insurance premiums, insurers are required to disclose to the policyholder when such parts are used in repairs.

Question 58:
What does California require from insurers offering both home and auto insurance policies?

A) They must offer a combined package at a discounted rate.
B) Separate agents must handle each type of policy.
C) Insurers are required to provide a discount if both are purchased.
D) There is no requirement to offer a discount for combined policies.

Correct Answer: C) Insurers are required to provide a discount if both are purchased.

Explanation:
California encourages consumers to bundle their insurance products by requiring insurers to offer discounts to customers who purchase both home and auto insurance policies from the same provider.

Question 59:
What protocol must California auto insurers follow when a policyholder is involved in an at-fault accident?

A) Immediate cancellation of the policy.
B) Increase in premiums at the next renewal.
C) Mandatory driver safety training.
D) Offer to settle any claims directly with third parties.

Correct Answer: B) Increase in premiums at the next renewal.

Explanation:
In California, auto insurers typically increase premiums at the next renewal following an at-fault accident, reflecting the higher risk associated with the policyholder.

Question 60:
What are the consequences for California insurance agents found guilty of misrepresentation?

A) Immediate loss of license.
B) Fines and potential suspension of their license.
C) Mandatory ethics training.
D) Both B and C.

Correct Answer: D) Both B and C.

Explanation:
California insurance agents found guilty of misrepresentation face fines, potential suspension of their license, and are often required to undergo mandatory ethics training to ensure compliance and integrity in their professional conduct.

Question 61:
Who enforces the insurance laws in California?

A) California Department of Motor Vehicles
B) California Bureau for Private Postsecondary Education
C) California State Police
D) California Department of Insurance

Correct Answer: D) California Department of Insurance

Explanation:
The California Department of Insurance is the primary state agency charged with overseeing and enforcing insurance laws in California. It regulates the insurance industry to ensure fairness, accountability, and compliance with all state regulations concerning insurance operations.

Question 62:
Which of the following is an insurer required to do when non-renewing a homeowner's policy in California?
A) Provide a 60-day notice
B) Offer an alternative policy
C) Transfer the policy to another insurer
D) Notify the mortgagee only

Correct Answer: A) Provide a 60-day notice

Explanation:
Under California law, insurers are required to provide a 60-day advance notice to homeowners when they decide not to renew a policy. This requirement ensures homeowners have adequate time to find alternative insurance coverage, safeguarding them against unexpected loss of coverage.

Question 63:
In California, which type of insurance must include coverage for newly acquired vehicles automatically for a certain period?
A) Life insurance

B) Property insurance
C) Health insurance
D) Auto insurance

Correct Answer: D) Auto insurance

Explanation:
California regulations stipulate that auto insurance policies must automatically cover any newly acquired vehicles for a specified period. This provision ensures that newly purchased or acquired vehicles are protected under the existing policy without immediate notification to the insurer.

Question 64:
Which coverage is mandatory for all employers in California?
A) Disability insurance
B) Liability insurance
C) Workers' compensation insurance
D) Life insurance

Correct Answer: C) Workers' compensation insurance

Explanation:
California mandates that all employers provide workers' compensation insurance. This coverage is essential as it protects employees who might get injured on the job by covering medical costs and lost wages, thus fulfilling employers' legal and ethical obligations.

Question 65:
What is the minimum amount of liability coverage for bodily injury per person required in California?
A) $5,000
B) $15,000
C) $25,000
D) $50,000

Correct Answer: B) $15,000

Explanation:
In California, the law requires that all drivers carry a minimum of $15,000 in liability coverage for bodily injury per person. This requirement ensures that adequate funds are available to cover medical expenses for injuries that the policyholder may cause to others in an auto accident.

Question 66:
Which authority regulates the licensing of insurance agents and brokers in California?
A) California Department of State
B) California Department of Public Safety
C) California Department of Insurance
D) California Licensing Board

Correct Answer: C) California Department of Insurance

Explanation:
The California Department of Insurance is responsible for regulating and licensing insurance agents and brokers in the state. It ensures that all practicing professionals meet the required standards and adhere to state laws, protecting consumers and maintaining the integrity of the insurance industry.

Question 67:
What must California drivers show proof of to register their vehicle?
A) Homeownership
B) Employment
C) Auto insurance
D) Health insurance

Correct Answer: C) Auto insurance

Explanation:
California law requires drivers to show proof of auto insurance when registering their vehicles. This policy ensures that all vehicles on the road have at least the minimum required liability coverage, providing financial protection in the event of an accident.

Question 68:
Which policy is a California insurer likely to recommend to a business owner to cover professional liability?
A) Umbrella policy
B) General liability policy
C) Errors and omissions insurance
D) Commercial property insurance

Correct Answer: C) Errors and omissions insurance

Explanation:

Errors and omissions insurance is recommended for business owners in California to cover professional liability, especially for those providing services or advice. This type of insurance protects against claims made by clients for negligent actions or inadequate work.

Question 69:
In the event of an insurance dispute in California, what is the first recommended method of resolution?
A) Court litigation
B) Arbitration
C) Mediation
D) Formal complaint to the DOI

Correct Answer: C) Mediation

Explanation:
In California, mediation is often recommended as the first method for resolving insurance disputes. This approach encourages both parties to discuss their issues in a facilitated environment to reach a mutual agreement, which can be more efficient and less adversarial than court proceedings.

Question 70:
What is a unique requirement for auto insurance policies in California regarding coverage options?
A) Offering international coverage
B) Providing uninsured motorist coverage
C) Annual rate adjustment
D) Monthly payment options

Correct Answer: B) Providing uninsured motorist coverage

Explanation:
California uniquely requires that all auto insurance policies offer uninsured motorist coverage as an option. This coverage protects insured drivers financially if they are involved in an accident with a driver who does not have insurance.

Question 71:
Who benefits directly from the California Life and Health Insurance Guarantee Association?
A) Insurance agents
B) Policyholders
C) Insurance companies
D) State government

Correct Answer: B) Policyholders

Explanation:
The California Life and Health Insurance Guarantee Association provides protection to policyholders in the event that their life or health insurance company becomes insolvent. This safeguard ensures that covered claims are still paid, even if the insurance company fails financially.

Question 72:
Which type of bond must California insurance agents maintain?
A) Performance bond
B) Bail bond
C) Surety bond
D) Savings bond

Correct Answer: C) Surety bond

Explanation:
California insurance agents are required to maintain a surety bond. This bond acts as a financial guarantee that the agent will adhere to the regulatory standards and ethical practices prescribed by the state.

Question 73:
What document must California insurance companies provide annually to policyholders?
A) Profit and loss statement
B) Coverage summary
C) Privacy policy
D) Marketing brochure

Correct Answer: C) Privacy policy

Explanation:
California insurers are mandated to provide their privacy policy to policyholders annually. This policy details how the insurance company collects, uses, and protects personal information, ensuring transparency and compliance with privacy regulations.

Question 74:
What does the California Automobile Assigned Risk Plan (CAARP) provide?
A) Special vehicle registrations
B) Auto insurance for high-risk drivers
C) Low-interest auto loans

D) Free vehicle inspections

Correct Answer: B) Auto insurance for high-risk drivers

Explanation:
The California Automobile Assigned Risk Plan (CAARP) offers auto insurance to drivers who are considered high-risk and have difficulty obtaining coverage through traditional channels. This program ensures that all drivers have access to mandatory auto insurance.

Question 75:
In California, what does a 'declarations page' in an insurance policy specify?
A) The policyholder's rights in court
B) The policy's coverage limits and premiums
C) A list of all past claims
D) Declarations of good health

Correct Answer: B) The policy's coverage limits and premiums

Explanation:
The declarations page of an insurance policy in California outlines crucial information including the coverage limits and the premiums. This page serves as a quick reference for policyholders to understand the key aspects of their insurance coverage.

Question 76:
What action must be taken by an insurer in California if it decides to withdraw a product from the market?
A) Notify the DOI at least 90 days in advance
B) Offer a similar product as a replacement
C) Buy back policies from current policyholders
D) Provide a public notice in major newspapers

Correct Answer: A) Notify the DOI at least 90 days in advance

Explanation:
When an insurer decides to withdraw a product from the market in California, they are required to notify the Department of Insurance at least 90 days in advance. This regulation allows the DOI to review the decision and ensures that policyholders are also given adequate notice.

Question 77:

How are insurance premiums for fire coverage in California's wildfire-prone areas influenced?
A) Premiums are typically lower
B) Premiums are based solely on property value
C) Premiums are typically higher
D) Premiums are subsidized by the state

Correct Answer: C) Premiums are typically higher

Explanation:
Due to the increased risk of fire damage in wildfire-prone areas, insurance premiums for properties in these regions of California are typically higher than in less risky areas.

Question 78:
What must California insurers provide for policyholders when issuing a new policy?
A) A welcome gift
B) A comprehensive policy review session
C) A policy summary or brochure
D) Access to the company's annual board meeting

Correct Answer: C) A policy summary or brochure

Explanation:
California insurers are required to provide a policy summary or brochure when issuing a new policy. This document helps policyholders understand the terms, coverage, and exclusions of their new insurance policy.

Question 79:
What is required from California insurance companies to ensure policyholder confidentiality?
A) Share information with third parties
B) Annual privacy training for all employees
C) Strict adherence to HIPAA guidelines
D) Regular security audits of IT systems

Correct Answer: D) Regular security audits of IT systems

Explanation:
To ensure the confidentiality and security of policyholder information, California insurance companies are required to conduct regular security audits of their IT systems. These audits help prevent unauthorized access to sensitive data and ensure compliance with privacy regulations.

Question 80:
Under what condition can a California insurance agent immediately lose their license?
A) Failing to meet sales quotas
B) Receiving low customer satisfaction scores
C) Committing insurance fraud
D) Changing insurance companies

Correct Answer: C) Committing insurance fraud

Explanation:
Committing insurance fraud is a serious offense in California, and it can lead to the immediate revocation of an insurance agent's license. This measure ensures the integrity of the insurance market and protects consumers from fraudulent activities.

Exam Preparation Strategies

Preparing for the Property and Casualty Insurance License Exam requires a structured approach to both learning the material and mastering the art of test-taking. Here are some strategies to help you effectively prepare for and succeed in your exam:

- ✓ **Develop a Study Schedule**: Create a realistic study schedule that breaks down the book's content into manageable sections, allowing ample time to understand each topic thoroughly. Allocate more time to complex chapters or those you are less familiar with. Consistency is key, so try to dedicate specific times of the day to your studies to build a routine.

- ✓ **Active Learning Techniques**: Engage actively with the material through summarizing, questioning, and applying the concepts. Use the flashcards included in this book to quiz yourself on key terms and definitions. This active engagement helps to reinforce memory retention and deepens your understanding of the material.

- ✓ **Practice with Purpose**: Make use of the multiple-choice questions provided in the second section to test your knowledge and get accustomed to the format of the exam questions. Analyze why certain answers are correct and others are not to improve your critical thinking skills, which are crucial during the exam.

- ✓ **Group Study Sessions**: If possible, organize study sessions with fellow exam takers. This can provide different perspectives on the material and help clarify doubts through discussion. Explaining concepts to others is also one of the best ways to solidify your own understanding.

- ✓ **Simulate Exam Conditions**: Periodically, simulate exam conditions by taking a timed practice test that includes questions from all book sections. This will familiarize you with the pressure of working within a time limit and help you identify areas where you might need more revision.

- ✓ **Review and Revise**: Regularly review your notes and summaries, especially for extensive or complex sections. This repetition will make it easier to recall information during the exam.

- ✓ **Stay Updated**: Keep an eye on any updates or changes in laws and regulations related to property and casualty insurance as your exam date approaches. This book covers the essentials, but insurance is a dynamic field, and being current can give you an edge.

- ✓ **Relax and Rest Before the Exam**: Ensure you get enough rest the night before the exam. A well-rested mind is more capable of recall and critical thinking. Try to relax and stay confident in the preparation you've done.

Following these strategies will enhance your ability to absorb the course material comprehensively and perform effectively on the exam. Remember, the goal of this book and your study efforts is not just to pass the exam but to lay a strong foundation for your insurance career.

Conclusion

As you approach the end of "Property and Casualty Insurance License Exam Prep: The Masterclass," it's important to reflect on your journey through the intricate landscape of property and casualty insurance. This book has been meticulously crafted to prepare you for the Property and Casualty Insurance License Exam and provide a comprehensive understanding of the insurance sector that will serve as a solid foundation for your career in the industry.

Throughout this guide, you've been equipped with clear-cut strategies, detailed explanations, and specific examples illuminating the core principles and advanced concepts of property and casualty insurance. Each section was designed to build upon the last, ensuring a cohesive and thorough understanding of the subject matter. From the basics of insurance policies to the complexities of state-specific regulations and advanced market dynamics, this book has covered a broad spectrum of topics for aspiring insurance professionals.

The book's structure was intentionally set to facilitate a progressive learning experience. Starting with fundamental concepts before moving into more detailed and specific discussions aimed to create a layered understanding. By now, you should feel confident in your grasp of the various types of insurance policies, the legal and regulatory environment in which they operate, and the risk management practices that underpin successful insurance undertakings.

One of the key elements of this book is the integration of practical, exam-focused content, such as multiple-choice questions and flashcards, which are designed to test and reinforce your knowledge. These tools are not just aids for passing the exam but are also valuable for applying theoretical knowledge in practical scenarios. The inclusion of state-specific questions ensures that you are prepared for particular nuances you may face, depending on where you plan to practice.

Moreover, the strategies outlined for effective study and exam preparation are intended to offer you the best possible chance at success. The approach recommended in this book—emphasizing active learning, regular practice, and engagement with the material—has been proven to enhance retention and understanding. These strategies are applicable in your immediate exam preparation and throughout your career as you continue to learn and grow professionally.

As you move forward, remember that the insurance field is dynamic and ever-evolving. Continuous learning and adaptation are key to maintaining expertise and excellence in any professional domain, especially in one as critical as insurance. The knowledge you have gained from this book provides a strong foundation, but the learning should not stop here. Keep abreast of new laws, policies, and practices that will inevitably arise as the market evolves and new risks emerge.

In closing, take pride in your effort to study this comprehensive guide. The dedication you've shown is indicative of your commitment to not only achieving success on the exam but also to your future role in protecting and advising the public through your work in insurance. Go forward confidently, equipped with knowledge, strategies, and insights to support your success in the Property and Casualty Insurance License Exam and beyond.

We hope you found "Property and Casualty Insurance License Exam Prep: The Masterclass" helpful and informative. If this guide was valuable in your exam preparation and you feel it might benefit others, we would appreciate it if you could take a moment to share your thoughts and experiences. Your feedback supports us and assists fellow learners in their journey towards becoming licensed professionals. Thank you for choosing this book, and we wish you all the best in your future endeavors in the insurance industry.

Blueprint Institute

Download here the bonus! Scar the QR code or go to the link below to download more than 1000 state-specific questions, printable flashcards and exam simulation

https://bit.ly/blueprintinstitutebonus

Made in United States
Troutdale, OR
09/27/2024

23198945R00071